STEPS
MATH

Collins Educational
An imprint of HarperCollinsPublishers

4b

Published by Collins Educational
An imprint of HarperCollins*Publishers*
77–85 Fulham Palace Road
Hammersmith
London
W6 8JB

First published 1994

ISBN 0 00 313841–0

Series Editor: Anne Woodman
Co-Editor: Paul Harling
Consultant Editor: Eric Albany

Illustrations: Kathy Baxendale (pages 28, 51), John Booth (pages
110, 111, 112, 113, 114), Juliet Breese (pages 21, 31, 46, 47, 61, 65,
70, 71, 119), Jean de Lemos (pages 4, 5, 9, 15, 17, 22, 24, 25, 26,
44, 83, 94, 100), Angela Lumley (pages 80, 81), Jenny Mumford
(pages 68, 69, 118), Archie Plumb (pages 10, 11, 19, 41, 42, 43, 82,
117), Malcolm Porter (pages 106, 121, 122), Polly Shields (78, 81,
104, 121, 122), Jane Taylor (page 70, 85), Peter Tucker (computer
graphics, pages 18, 20, 23, 30, 36, 43, 59, 88, 89, 102, 103, 105),
Martin Ursell (pages 33, 34, 60, 92, 93, 96, 115).

Photographs: all Martin Sookias, apart from: British Aerospace
Airbus Limited (page 16), Hong Kong Government (page 6), Image
Bank (page 110), Letraset (pages 27, 84, 85), Mary Evans Picture
Library (page 28). Cover: Image Bank.

Design and typesetting: Alex Tucker, PGT Design, Oxford.

Printing: Scotprint, Musselburgh, Scotland.

The authors and publishers would like to thank NES Arnold and
Texas Instruments for lending mathematical equipment for
photographs.

STEPS ■ ■ ■ ■ ■ ■ ■ ■ ■ 4b
MATHEMATICS

Contents

The coloured blocks at the top of a page show you that the work is mainly about:

number   algebra   shape and space   handling data   measurement

A box like this at the top of a page tells you what you will need. We expect that you will always have a ruler, pencil, eraser and colouring materials so they aren't shown in the boxes.

balance scales, rice, plastic bag

Multiplication tables

completed copy of RM 2, calculator

1 Write the missing products from these parts of a completed multiplication square.

The first one is started for you.

Afterwards, check your answers using your completed square on RM 2.

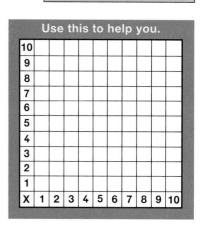

Use this to help you.

a

6	y
4	6
x	3

$x \longrightarrow 2$

$y \longrightarrow$

b

x		
28	35	y
24		

c

x	56
48	
y	45

d

21	y	
x	18	24

e

40		
x		
24	y	30

f

18		30
15	x	25
	y	

g

28	x	42	y	56
			48	z

h

x			
27	y	45	54
24			z
			42

i

		x
	42	49
	36	42
	y	30

j

15	x	25
		y
	12	z

k

16	20	x	28
y		18	z
8			

2 Alex took this cross from the multiplication square. When she added the numbers in this way she found that each total was double the number in the middle of the cross.

$4 + 8 = 12$

$9 + 3 = 12$

$6 \times 2 = 12$

Does this always happen?

Choose 10 other crosses and write about what you find.

	9	
4	6	8
	3	

CHALLENGE

Find out what happens if you start with larger crosses instead.

Square numbers

1 Copy and continue this pattern until you have drawn the 6th square number. Use grid paper if it helps.

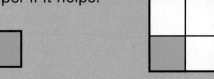

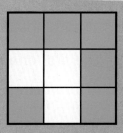

1st square number = 1
1 x 1 = 1
1

2nd square number = 4
2 x 2 = 4
1 + 3 = 4

3rd square number = 9
3 x 3 = 9
1 + 3 + 5 = 9

2 **a** Copy and complete this arrow diagram.

   b Design arrow diagrams for the 7th, 8th, 9th and 10th square numbers.

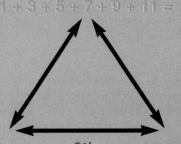

1 + 3 + 5 + 7 + 9 + 11 = _____

6 x 6 = _____   6th square number = _____

3 **a** Copy and complete this difference pattern using the same colours.

| 1 | 4 | 9 | 16 | 25 | 36 | 49 | 64 | 81 | 100 |

   b Write what you think the green numbers stand for.

   c Write what you think the red numbers stand for.

CHALLENGE

- 100 is the 10th square number.
- Decide how to find what square numbers these are.
- Use a calculator if you want to.

169   441   625   1024

2

Starting on factors

You can draw line-and-dot diagrams like these to show the factors of 18.

$9 \times 2 = 18$

$18 \times 1 = 18$

$6 \times 3 = 18$

Set of factors of 18 = {1, 2, 3, 6, 9, 18}

1 **a** Make 3 line-and-dot diagrams to show the factors of **12**.
  b Write the set of factors of 12.

2 Do the same to show the factors of **20**.

3 Write the set of factors for these numbers.

  a 15   **b** 32   **c** 7   **d** 16   **e** 28   **f** 11   **g** 30   **h** 27

4 Copy and complete these diagrams.
  Two more factors go in the inner region of **a**.

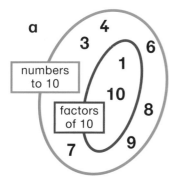

a

numbers to 10

factors of 10

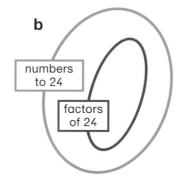

b

numbers to 24

factors of 24

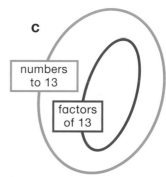

c

numbers to 13

factors of 13

5 These numbers have more than 8 factors. Try to find them all.
  Use a calculator if you want to.

  a 48   **b** 60   **c** 36   **d** 80

CHALLENGE

- Four of these numbers have an odd number of factors.
- Find them. ■ Write what is special about them.

Do-the-same machines ■ ■ ■ ■

1 This is a 1-operation function machine.

It is a (×8) machine.

Copy and complete its input/output table.

2 This is a 2-operation function machine.

It is a (×2) then (×4) machine.

Copy and complete its input/output table.

3 Write what you notice about the OUT numbers in **1** and **2** .

4 Copy and complete these pairs of 'do-the-same' machines.

a

5 → (×---) → 50

5 → (×5) → (×---) → 50

b

4 → (×---) → 36

4 → (×3) → (×---) → 36

c

10 → (×---) → 60

10 → (×---) → (×---) → 60

d

3 → (×---) → 60

3 → (×4) → (×---) → 60

e

7 → (×---) → 700

7 → (×---) → (×10) → 700

f

6 → (×---) → 180

6 → (×5) → (×---) → 180

5 Design a 1-operation machine to replace each of these.

a → (×9) → (×10) →

b → (×4) → (×40) →

c → (×10) → (×20) →

d → (×8) → (×8) →

e → (×5) → (×8) →

f → (×12) → (×2) →

4

Here are two 2-operation machines with the same IN numbers.

IN	MIDDLE	OUT
1		
3		
4		
7		
8		

6 a Write the MIDDLE and OUT numbers for machine A.
   b Write the MIDDLE and OUT numbers for machine B.
   c Write why the OUT numbers for machines A and B are the same.

7 Copy and complete these pairs of do-the-same machines.
   Use a calculator if you need to.

a
3 → ×2 → ×8 →
3 → ×4 → ×--- → 48

b
5 → ×9 → ×--- → 90
5 → ×--- → 90

c
6 → ×--- → ×2 → 120
6 → ×4 → ×--- → 120

d
9 → ×6 → ×--- → 270
9 → ×3 → ×--- → 270

8 Complete the 2-operation machines
   to replace this 1-operation machine.   ×90

a → ×90 → ◯ →
b → ×9 → ◯ →
c → ×30 → ◯ →
d → ×2 → ◯ →
e → ◯ → ×6 →
f → ◯ → ×5 →

9 Check each machine in 8 by feeding 2 in to it.
   Decide how to record your results.

CHALLENGE
Design different machines to replace a ×60 machine.

Areas and perimeters

1 Estimate, then try to work out the area of each rectangle in this cut-up picture. Use your ruler to help.

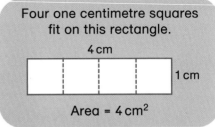

Four one centimetre squares fit on this rectangle.

4 cm

1 cm

Area = 4 cm²

2 Write down how you found the areas.

3 Afterwards, check the area of each rectangle with the transparent grid.

4 Copy and complete this table for rectangles **a** to **k**.

rectangle	length	width	area
a	8 cm		24 cm²

5 Complete this sentence: 'The easiest way to find the area of a rectangle is ...'

6 Show how you work out the perimeter of each rectangle **a** to **f**.

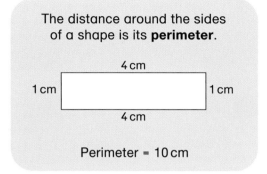

The distance around the sides of a shape is its **perimeter**.

Perimeter = 10 cm

7 On RM A draw squares with the same area as each of these shapes.

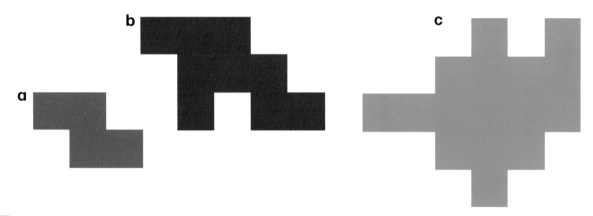

8 Write the perimeter of each square beside it.

9 Draw squares with perimeters of these lengths.

a 24 cm   **b** 36 cm   **c** 40 cm   **d** 28 cm

10 Complete this table for squares with sides from 1 cm to 10 cm.

length of sides	perimeter
1 cm	4 cm
2 cm	

11 Copy and complete this: 'You can find the perimeter of a square by ... or by... .'

CHALLENGE

On RM A, show that you can construct 5 rectangles each with a perimeter of 22 cm.

Surface areas ■ ■

Centicubes, scissors,
1 cm squared paper (RMA)

1 Use Centicubes to make a cube
of this size.

- Length   3 cm
- Breadth 3 cm
- Height   3 cm

2 Copy and complete these.

a Surface area of cube = ... cm².
b I worked out the surface area by ... .

> You can find the surface area
> of a rectangular box
> by totalling the areas
> of all the faces.

3 Use the same number of cubes
to make a cuboid of this size:

- Length 9 cm   ■ Breadth 3 cm   ■ Height 1 cm

4 Copy and complete these.

a Surface area of cuboid = ... cm².
b I worked out the surface area by ... .
c The difference in surface area between the cube
and the cuboid is ... cm².

5 Try to work out the surface area of these **without** using cubes.
Afterwards, check with cubes if you want to.

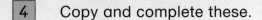

a   b   c

6 Show how you can find the surface area of each box.

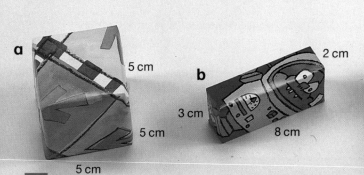

a

5 cm

5 cm

5 cm

b

3 cm

8 cm

2 cm

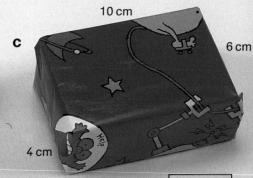

c

10 cm

6 cm

4 cm

STEPS 4b:2

7 Write the way you think best to find the surface areas of these.

  a cubes   **b** cuboids

CHALLENGE

> If you make a cube and cuboid with the same number of Centicubes, the cube always has the smaller surface area.

Decide how to show if this is true:

REVISION   NETS OF CUBOIDS

1 Use Centicubes to make the cuboid for which this is the net.

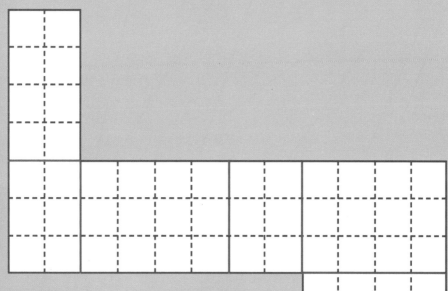

2 Afterwards, copy the net on to 1 cm squared paper.

3 Cut it out and fold along the bold lines.
Is it the same size as the cuboid you made?

Measuring angles

Ask your teacher which would be
a good protractor for you to use.

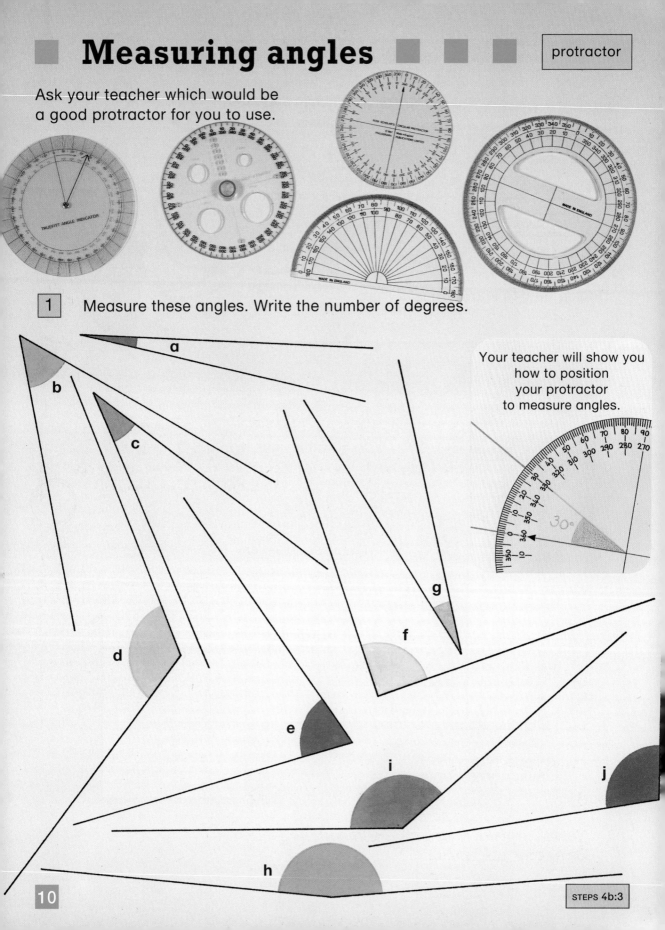

1   Measure these angles. Write the number of degrees.

Your teacher will show you
how to position
your protractor
to measure angles.

a

b

c

d

e

f

g

h

i

j

Drawing angles ■ ■ ■ ■

How to draw an angle of 70°

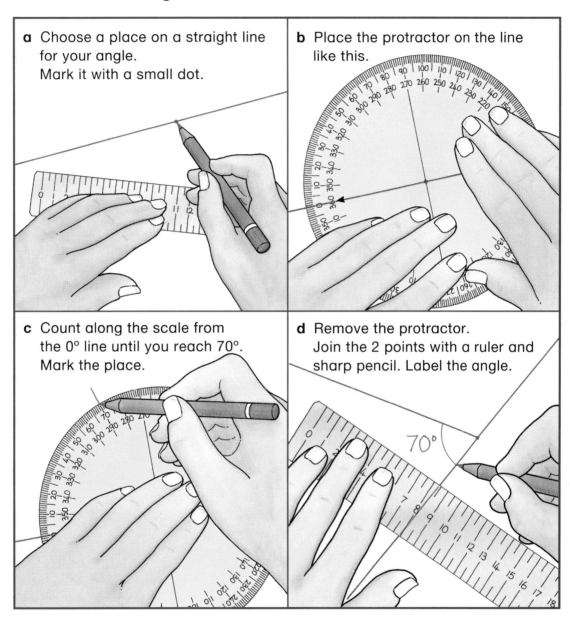

a Choose a place on a straight line for your angle.
Mark it with a small dot.

b Place the protractor on the line like this.

c Count along the scale from the 0° line until you reach 70°.
Mark the place.

d Remove the protractor.
Join the 2 points with a ruler and sharp pencil. Label the angle.

70°

---

1 Draw these angles.

a 40°   **b** 90°   **c** 100°   **d** 120°   **e** 150°   **f** 170°

2 Choose different sizes of angles to draw.
Draw and label them.

Percentages and fractions

Mr and Mrs Shah bought 100 comics to sell in their shop.

1 Write the number of comics left each day if they sell these amounts.

   a 12% on Monday   **b** 25% on Tuesday   **c** 10% on Wednesday
   d 8% on Thursday   **e** 20% on Friday   **f** 22% on Saturday
   g 3% on Sunday

2 Write the fraction of comics sold on these days.
   Choose one of these fractions each time:

   a Tuesday   **b** Wednesday   **c** Friday
   d Thursday to Saturday   **e** Saturday and Sunday   **f** Monday to Friday.

3 Write this list of percentages and fractions in order of size, smallest first.

CHALLENGE

Design a workcard, for others to try out, which
gives practice in percentages and fractions.

Percentages of 50

1 Check that there are 50 sweets in this array.

> 12 out of 50 sweets are yellow.
> This is the same as 24 out of 100.
> So 24% are yellow.

2 Write what percentage of the sweets are:

a    b   c   d

e not   f not   g not   h not

CHALLENGE

Write 9 more sentences like this for other pairs of colours.

42% are speckled and red.

Percentages of 200

This pattern is made from 200 cubes.
10 out of 200 cubes are orange.
This is the same as 5 out of 100.
So 5% of the cubes are orange.

1 Write how many cubes are:

- **a** orange
- **b** blue
- **c** yellow
- **d** black
- **e** red
- **f** green.

2 Check that your answers to **1** total 200 cubes.

3 Write 5 more sentences like this, one for each colour.

5% of the cubes are orange.

4 Write 5 more sentences like this, one for each colour.

95% of the cubes are not orange.

5 Choose a grid and colours to design a symmetrical pattern from 200 squares.

Write about the percentage of each colour used.

CHALLENGE

- Draw grids like this on squared paper.
- Colour them in different ways.
- Write the percentage of colours used on each grid.

14

STEPS 4b:4

Your favourite way

1. Choose **your** favourite way to find the totals of these.

   Remember to think 'the answer will be about ...' first.

   a 417 + 590   b 507 + 595   c 761 + 394
   d 647 + 552   e 856 + 270   f 967 + 239

2. You can make 10 different totals by adding pairs of these numbers together.
   Try to find them all.

   789   829
   258   443   670

3. Work out how many you need to add to each number to total 1000. Show what you do.

   a 435   b 505   c 681   d 228

CHALLENGE

There are 10 different ways to complete this.

4 ■ 7 + 5 ■ 3 = 1000
True or false? Investigate.

467 + 5 3 = 1000

Long distance flights ■ ■ ■

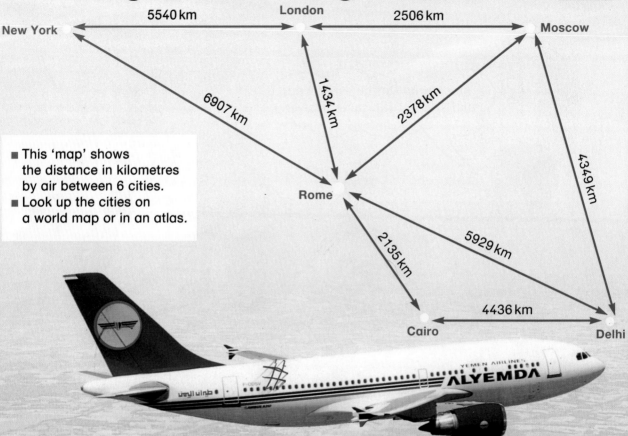

5540 km

London

2506 km

New York

Moscow

6907 km

1434 km

2378 km

4349 km

Rome

■ This 'map' shows
the distance in kilometres
by air between 6 cities.
■ Look up the cities on
a world map or in an atlas.

2135 km

5929 km

4436 km

Cairo

Delhi

1 Work out the distances travelled on these flights.

   a London to Cairo via Rome   **b** Moscow to Cairo via Rome
   c New York to Moscow via London   **d** Rome to New York via London
   e Cairo to New York via Rome   **f** Delhi to London via Rome

2 Work out the distance travelled on a return flight between these cities.

   a London and Rome   **b** Cairo and Delhi
   c Delhi and Moscow   **d** Moscow and Rome

CHALLENGE

■ Design a similar 'map' for these cities.   ■ Use an atlas to help.
■ Write questions you can ask about it and the answers.

London to Bombay	7205 km	Geneva to Bombay	6725 km
London to Geneva	748 km	Berlin to Geneva	876 km
London to Washington	5915 km	Berlin to London	934 km
Bombay to Berlin	6298 km		

Here are two
I've done.

1 34 + 2 60 + 5 ☰ *399.*

1 436 + 502 ☰ *1938.*

1   Make different totals using
the 9 arrowed keys each time.

2   Keep a record of each
example you find.

3   Write headings like these
and put some additions under each heading.

a   Totals from
0 to 999

b   Totals from
1000 to 1999

c   Totals from
2000 to 2999

d   Totals from
3000 to 3999

e   Totals from
4000 to 4999

f   Totals from
5000 to 5999

g   Totals from
6000 to 6999

4   Compare your results with others.

Who found
the largest total?

Polygon hunt

1 Which shapes from A to P are:

   a triangles   **b** quadrilaterals
   c pentagons   **d** hexagons?

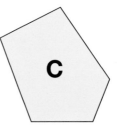

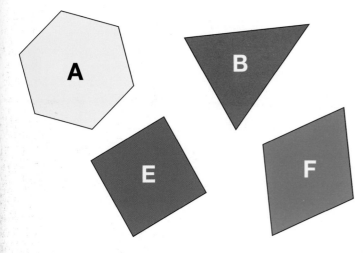

2 Which shape is:

   a an equilateral triangle
   b a rhombus
   c a parallelogram
   d a trapezium
   e a regular pentagon?

3 Which shapes have:

   a all angles equal
   b 2 pairs of parallel sides
   c all sides of different lengths
   d at least 1 acute angle?

4 On RM G draw:

   a a parallelogram
   b a right-angled triangle
   c a pentagon with 3 right angles
   d a trapezium with 2 right angles
   e a hexagon with no right angles.

> **CHALLENGE**
> Try to draw 5 hexagons, each with
> a different number of right angles.

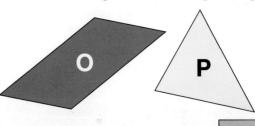

Constructing triangles

This is one way to construct a triangle with sides of 4 cm, 5 cm and 3 cm.

Rule a line the length of one side.

Set the compasses to the length of another side.

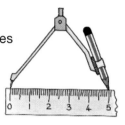

Draw an arc like this.

Set the compasses to the length of the third side.

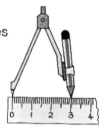

Draw a second arc like this, crossing the first.

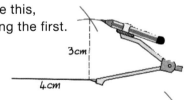

Complete the triangle like this.

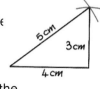

Check the length of the triangle's sides.

1 Follow the instructions to construct a triangle like the one in the box.

2 Construct these triangles.

- **a** 4 cm 7 cm 9 cm
- **b** 7 cm 6 cm 5 cm
- **c** 8 cm 5 cm 7 cm
- **d** 9 cm 10 cm 4 cm

3 Using compasses, contruct:

- **a** an equilateral triangle
- **b** an isosceles triangle
- **c** a scalene triangle.

4 Write the length of the sides on your triangles from **3**.

CHALLENGE

Show how you can construct **10 different** scalene triangles with sides of these lengths.

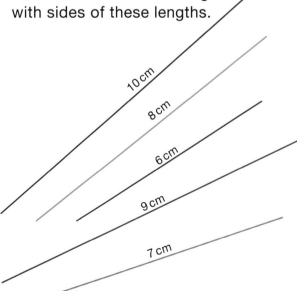

10 cm
8 cm
6 cm
9 cm
7 cm

Triangles from angles

These angles of 60°
can be turned
into triangles
by adding a third side.

right-hand
corner

left-hand
corner

60°   60°

1 Use your protractor to draw triangles with
a **right-hand corner** of this size.
The sides can be any length.

a   **b**   **c**   **d**

40°   110°   70°   90°

2 Draw triangles with a **left-hand corner** of this size.
All the sides should be shorter than 10 cm.

a   **b**   **c**   **d**

50°   20°   80°   130°

3 Decide the best way to copy and complete these triangles.

a
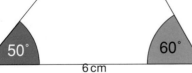
50°   60°
6 cm

b
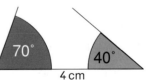
70°   40°
4 cm

c
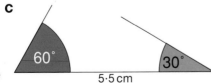
60°   30°
5·5 cm

d
40°   20°
6·4 cm

e
100°   30°
8·2 cm

f
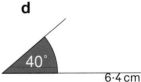
20°   130°
4·9 cm

Addition in your head

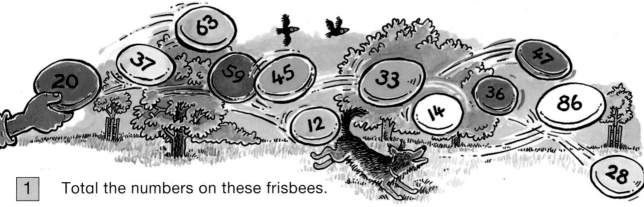

1   Total the numbers on these frisbees.

     a red frisbees   **b** blue frisbees   **c** green frisbees
     d white frisbees   **e** yellow frisbees   **f** purple frisbees
     g 2nd and 6th frisbees   **h** 5th and 9th frisbees   **i** 4th and 12th frisbees

2

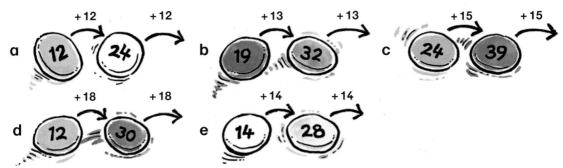

3   One way to complete ■ ■ + 25 = ■ 9 is like this: **34 + 25 = 59**

     Find and record the 6 other ways you can complete it.

4   Show that you can complete this
     in 8 different ways.

     ■ 7 + ■ 2 = 99

5   Show that you can complete this
     in 7 different ways.

     ■ 9 + 15 = ■ 4

CHALLENGE

- Use any shapes you like.
- Put 2-digit numbers which total 100
  at the corners of the shapes.
- Make up more examples like these.

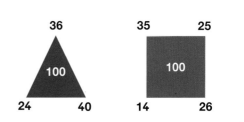

Total scores

Work out the answers in your head.

> The winner's the one with the highest total score for the two games. Let's see who's the winner in our group.

Name	Game1	Game2	Total score
Sue	54	40	
Robert	37	45	
Jimmy	43	36	
Ravinder	39	51	
Nina	27	65	
Lai Lang	71	28	

1 Write the total score for each player.

2 Write who won.

> I've hidden some of the scores for our group with counters.

Name	Game1	Game2	Total score
Chas	24	●	77
Dorian	59	●	86
Anna	●	29	100
Tara	●	34	69
David	48	●	95
Martin	●	47	73
Gopal	35	●	81

3 Work out the missing score for each player on the board on the left.

4 Decide scores for everyone on the board on the right.

RULES

- Nobody had a score ending in 0.
- Nobody had the same score in Game 1 **and** Game 2.
- Nobody scored the same as other players.

Name	Game 1	Game 2	Total score
Bob			75
Annie			72
Malik			81
Susan			65
Eric			89
Lucy			98
Frank			93

Totals and differences

Work out the answers in your head.

1 On the star, find the difference
between the numbers
in the triangles coloured:

    a red   **b** blue   **c** green
    d yellow **e** purple **f** white.

2 Now find the difference between
these numbers on the star.

    a two highest
    b two lowest
    c highest and lowest
    d two highest even
    e highest and lowest odd

3 Write the next three numbers in these sequences.

a

— 76 — 65 — 54 —

b

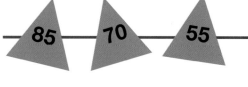

— 85 — 70 — 55 —

c

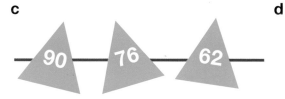

— 90 — 76 — 62 —

d

— 99 — 81 — 63 —

4 One way to complete 96 - ■ ■ = ■ ■ is like this. $96 - 45 = 51$

Find and record 7 other ways.

5 Show that you can complete this in 7 different ways. ■4 – 17 = ■7

CHALLENGE

- Use 2-digit numbers only.
- Use at least one '+' and '–' sign every time.
- Make different answers from 50 to 60.

$23 + 46 - 11 = 58$

$50 + 40 + 25 - 55 = 60$

Lawn lengths

This is the plan of a lawn.
One weekend, Matthew trimmed the edges.
He worked clockwise from A to B to C on Saturday
morning, and from C to D to E in the afternoon.
The following morning he trimmed from E to F to A.

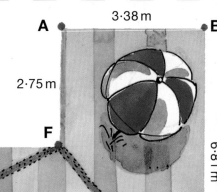
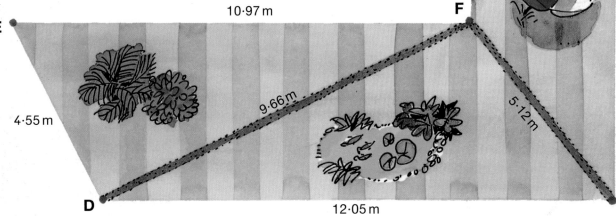

A — 3·38 m — B

2·75 m

6·81 m

F

E

10·97 m

4·55 m

9·66 m

5·12 m

D — 12·05 m — C

1 Find the total distance he trimmed on:

    a Saturday morning   **b** Saturday afternoon   **c** Sunday morning
    d Saturday morning and afternoon   **e** Saturday and Sunday.

2 Afterwards, he walked anticlockwise from B to check his work.
   Find the total distance he walked from:

    a B to A to F   **b** F to E to D   **c** D to C to B.

3 If he uses the paths, how far will he walk from:

    a D to F to A   **b** C to F to A   **c** D to F to C?

4   **a** 8·54 m   **b** 9·14 m   **c** 10·14 m   **d** 12·47 m   **e** 14·57 m
      +5·13 m   + 7·38 m   + 6·84 m   + 5·45 m   + 4·68 m

      ————   ————   ————   ————   ————

CHALLENGE

*I can't use the same path
more than once
on each journey.*

Find all the different ways Matthew can walk
from A to D and the distance he will walk each time.

24

Subtracting lengths

Show how you work out your answers.

1 This is Matthew's family.
Show how you can use this arrow
5 more times to compare their heights.

Mum is 0·71 m taller than Lisa →

Dad   Mum   Lisa   Matthew
1·95 m 1·56 m 0·85 m   1·29 m

2 Lisa made 18 m of decorations
for her party.
Write how much she will have left each time
if she cuts lengths off in this order.

a 1·25 m for the porch
b 1·60 m for the hallway
c 2·25 m for the kitchen
d 9·50 m for the living room

3 Show how you can complete this sentence in 6 different ways.
The _____ needed ___ m less of the decorations than the _____ .

4 Dad bought 12 m of wood
to make a dog kennel.
Write how much he will have left each time
if he cuts lengths off in this order.

a 2·92 m   b 3·25 m   c 3·25 m   d 2·07 m

5
a 9·75 m	b 9·64 m	c 14·38 m	d 15·35 m	e 17·36 m
− 6·14 m	− 5·47 m	−10·74 m	− 8·89 m	− 9·49 m
_____	_____	_____	_____	_____

CHALLENGE
Write a story for this subtraction. 20 m − 3·15 m − 4·75 m − 5·07 m

All kinds of lengths ■ ■ ■ ■ ■

Show how you work out the answers.

> **You can write the same measurements in different ways.**
>
> 34mm = 3cm 4mm = 3·4cm
> 156cm = 1m 56cm = 1·56m

1 Draw lines 1·4 cm longer than these.
Under each one, write its length
in millimetres.

a ────────────────────

b ────

c ──────────

d ──────────────────

e ──────────────────────────────

f ─────────────────────────────

g ──────────────────────────────────

2 Work out what length will be left if 45 cm is cut off these
lengths of wrapping paper.

a 94 cm   **b** 1·7 m   **c** 2 m 20 cm   **d** 4·04 m

3 Write the difference between the length and width
of each of these classrooms.

a

Our classroom is 10·58 m long. The width is 8 m 22 cm.

b

The length of our room is 12 m 5 cm. It is 10·45 m wide.

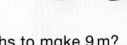

4 What do you have to add to strips of these lengths to make 9 m?

a 3 m 45 cm   **b** 5·56 m   **c** 250 cm   **d** 4·02 m

5 If you cut four 10 cm strips and four 8 cm strips from a length
of balsa wood which is 1·5 m long, how much will be left?

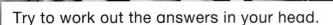

Try to work out the answers in your head.

1   Copy and complete the purple table.

1476 – 1	=	1475	
1476 – 10	=		
1476 – 100	=		
1476 – 1000	=		

2   Design a table like the purple one for each of these.

     a 5489   **b** 6512   **c** 7777   **d** 4000

3   Copy and complete the blue table.

5463 – 5000 =	463	
463 –	=	63
63 –	=	3
3 –	=	0

4   Design a table like the blue one for each of these.

     a 2579   **b** 1986   **c** 4752   **d** 9345

5   Starting with 5000 each time, complete these tables.

a
5000 – 2	=	
____ – 20	=	
____ – 200	=	
____ – 2000	=	

b
____ – 5	=	
____ – 50	=	
____ – 500	=	
____ – 5000	=	

c
____ – 4	=	
____ – 40	=	
____ – 400	=	
____ – 4000	=	

CHALLENGE

- Continue this pattern as far as you can.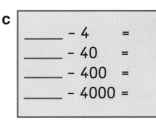
- Make up your own ⤳ patterns.

Royal connections

These are the 6 monarchs who reigned before Queen Elizabeth II.

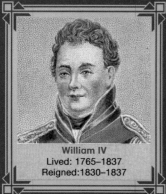

William IV
Lived: 1765–1837
Reigned: 1830–1837

Victoria
Lived: 1819–1901
Reigned: 1837–1901

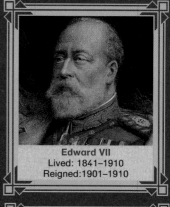

Edward VII
Lived: 1841–1910
Reigned: 1901–1910

George V
Lived: 1865–1936
Reigned: 1910–1936

Edward VIII
Lived: 1894–1972
Reigned: 1936

George VI
Lived: 1895–1952
Reigned: 1936–1952

1 Complete a scroll like this for the monarchs.
   Keep a record of how you work out your answers.

2 Elizabeth II became Queen in 1952
   at the age of 26.
   When was she born?

3 On your paper strip, copy and continue
   this time line to show all the monarchs
   up to the present day.

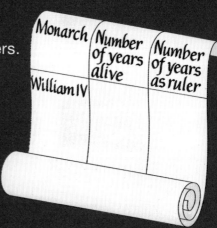

Monarch	Number of years alive	Number of years as ruler
William IV		

1830 1837   1901
William IV   Victoria
        (Scale: 2mm represents 1 year)

These coins were made at the Royal Mint which makes all British coins.

a
1937

b
1900

c
1858

d
1945

e
1934

4 Write the reign in which each coin was minted.

5 Work out how many years ago each coin was minted.

f
1887

g
1907

h
1834

Investigate why there are no coins for Edward VIII.

6 Draw an arrow diagram like this starting with the other 5 monarchs before Elizabeth II.

Try to work out the answers in your head.

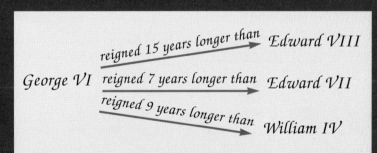

George VI
— reigned 15 years longer than → Edward VIII
— reigned 7 years longer than → Edward VII
— reigned 9 years longer than → William IV

7 Find the answers to these.

a 3146 – 1029   b 4470 – 2557   c 8348 – 3770   d 9132 – 6485

8 Show that you can make 6 different subtractions by finding the difference between pairs of these numbers.

5137

9179

7098

3018

Congruent shapes

1 Copy and complete this arrow diagram to show that there are 8 pairs of congruent shapes below.

> is congruent to
>
> a ↔
>
> b ↔

> If objects are identical in shape and size, they are **congruent** to each other.
> These combs are **congruent** to each other.

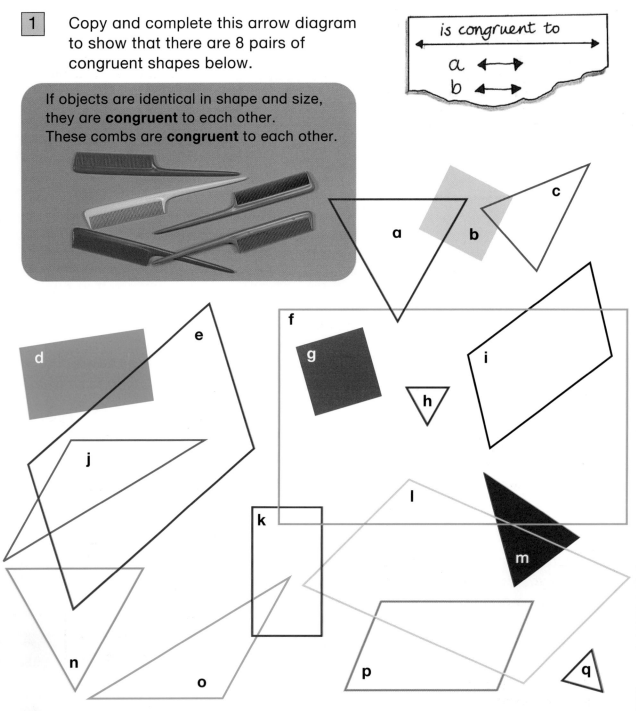

2 Draw a shape congruent to the one with no partner.

3 Draw 3 more pairs of congruent shapes.

Pinboard investigation

This is what Dan thinks.

This is what Jayesh thinks.

There are only
16 different quadrilaterals
on the 3 × 3 pinboard.

You can make
18 different quadrilaterals
on the 3 x 3 pinboard.

This is a trapezium
we found.

1 Find out which statement is true.
Record your answers on RM K.

RULE

No congruent quadrilaterals are allowed.

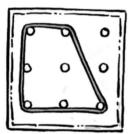

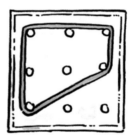

If you find this ...   ... others like these are not allowed.

2 On your pinboard, find as many different triangles
as you can **congruent** to the one on the right.
Record on another copy of RM K.

RULE

Each triangle should be
in a new position.

Here is one way.
There are lots more!

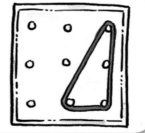

Similar shapes

1 Construct an equilateral triangle
congruent to this one.

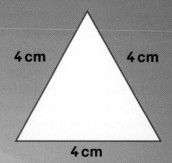

4 cm   4 cm

4 cm

2 Construct 3 triangles **similar**
to it with sides of these lengths.

a twice as long
b one-and-a-half times as long
c half as long

Look on page 19
if you have forgotten
what to do.

3 Construct an isosceles triangle
congruent to this one.

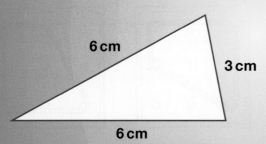

6 cm

3 cm

6 cm

4 Construct 4 triangles similar
to it with sides of these lengths.

a twice as long
b half as long
c one-and-a-half times as long
d a third as long

5 Write the lengths of the sides on the 4 triangles you drew in **4** .

6 **a** Construct a scalene triangle and write the length of its sides.
  b Draw several similar triangles and write the length of the sides
  on each one.

CHALLENGE

- Find a way to construct
  pairs of similar
  quadrilaterals.

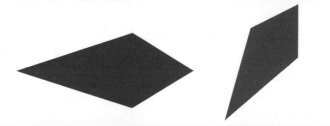

- These kites are similar.

Multitrack routes

Salma and Anthony are playing their version
of the game **Multitrack**.

1 Can you complete a route for each of them?

> **Don't travel on the same track more than once.**
> **Don't multiply by 1.**

■ Salma
■ Anthony

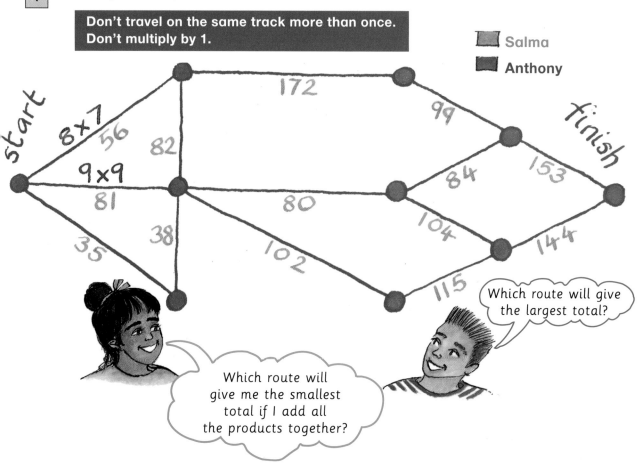

Which route will give
the largest total?

Which route will
give me the smallest
total if I add all
the products together?

2 Salma decides to pick a number from the track to see how many
different pairs of factors she can find.
She chooses 144 and writes:

$$144 = 1 \times 144$$
$$144 = 2 \times 72$$
$$144 = 3 \times$$

Can you complete her list?

3 Anthony chooses 80. How many pairs should he find?

4 This is the start of Amy
and Robin's **Multitrack**.
Decide how to complete it
so that it has 16 sections
of track.

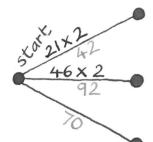

This is a **×2 Multitrack**
only. Use numbers
between **20** and **200**.

More Multitrack ■ ■ ■ ■ ■ ■

Now Marie and Tara are designing their own **Multitrack**.

1 Copy their track. Complete it so that there is a different multiplication on each track.

61 × 6

start

finish

2 Work out the answers to the multiplications, starting with the smallest product.

3 Which route will give the largest and smallest totals on their **Multitrack** if they add the products?

Don't travel on the same track more than once.

CHALLENGE

■ Design your own **Multitrack** to give practice in multiplying 2-digit by 1-digit numbers.

■ Make sure you can answer the problems before trialling it.

Shape cards

1 Copy and complete these shape database cards.
Look for clues to help you.

a

Name of shape: Cu
Number of faces:
Edges:
Vertices:
Shape of faces:
Is it a prism?
Examples: Brick

b

6
12
8
square

c

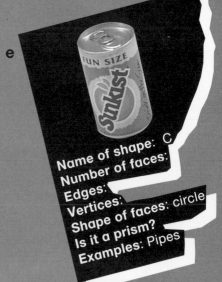

Name of shape: Triangular pr
Number of faces: 5
Edges:
Vertices:
Shape of faces:
Is it a prism?
Examples: Roof

d

Name of shape: Square-based
Number of faces: 5
Edges:
Vertices:
Shape of faces: Squ
Is it a prism?
Examples: Egyptian

e

Name of shape: C
Number of faces:
Edges:
Vertices:
Shape of faces: circle
Is it a prism?
Examples: Pipes

f

Name of shape: He   prism
Number of faces:
Edges:
Vertices: 12
Shape of faces: oblong and
Is it a prism?
Examples:

CHALLENGE

Imagine and draw what
these shapes would look like
if you opened them out
to form nets.

Constructing tetrahedra

compasses, card, scissors, glue

This is one way to construct a tetrahedron with 4 congruent faces.

1 On card, draw an equilateral triangle with compasses set at 5 cm.

See page 19 if you can't remember what to do.

2 Draw a congruent equilateral triangle.

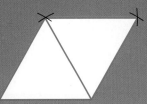

3 Draw a third triangle.

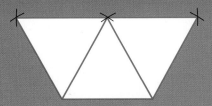

4 Draw a fourth triangle to complete the net.

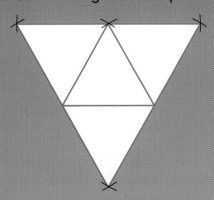

5 Draw tabs and then cut out.

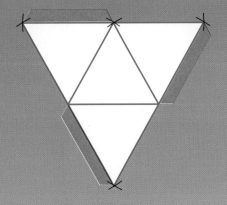

6 Score, fold and glue.

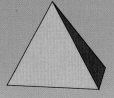

CHALLENGE

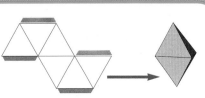

- Use compasses set at 4 cm to draw this net for a hexahedron. Add tabs.

- Construct a congruent hexahedron from a **different** net.

Design a prism

Choose materials to design
a triangular prism which will be
a sensible size to hold either:

These are triangular prisms.

a

10 new crayons

b

a glue stick

c

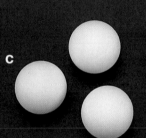

3 table-tennis balls

d

or 10 new pencils.

RULES

- The contents should fit snugly.
- The container should have an opening lid.

CHALLENGE

Construct a triangular prism with end faces which are:

- scalene triangles
- isosceles triangles.

Ordered pairs ■ ■ ■ ■ ■ ■ ■

You can describe or plot a point on a graph using co-ordinates.

Co-ordinates are sometimes called **ordered pairs** because it's important to read them in the right order: **the number on the horizontal axis before the number on the vertical axis.**

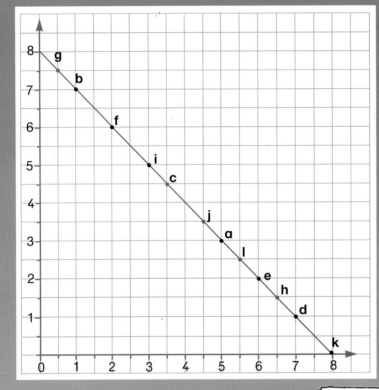

Some points are plotted on this straight line graph.

1 Complete this list to show ordered pairs for the black points.

$$a \rightarrow (5, \quad)$$
$$b \rightarrow$$

2 Write what is the same about the ordered pairs in ☐1☐.

3 Complete this list to show ordered pairs for the red points.

$$g \rightarrow (\tfrac{1}{2}, \quad)$$
$$h \rightarrow$$

4 Write what is the same about all the ordered pairs in ☐3☐.

5 Copy and continue this pattern.

$$0 + 8 = 8$$
$$\tfrac{1}{2} + 7\tfrac{1}{2} = 8$$
$$1 +$$

STEPS 4b:13

More ordered pairs

5 mm squared paper (RM C)

1   On RM C, draw axes and number them as shown below.

2   Mark in **blue** all the points which show pairs of whole numbers which add up to 10.

3   Mark in **red** all the points which show pairs of numbers with halves which add up to 10.

4   Write what you notice about the red and blue points.

Graph showing pairs of numbers which add to 10.

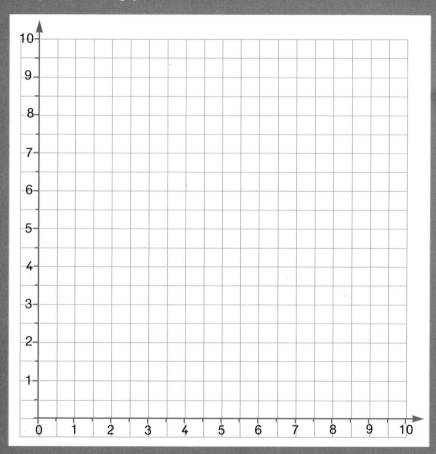

CHALLENGE

■ Choose a squared paper.

■ Draw a graph to show numbers with quarters in them which add up to 5.

1 Continue this pattern of ordered pairs for the x 2 table.
Stop when you reach (10, 20).
(0,0) (1,2) (2,4) ...

2 Plot the ordered pairs on the graph on RM 39.
The first 2 have been done for you.

3 Afterwards, join the points with
a sharp pencil and ruler.

4 Write the ordered pairs for the x 4 table
in the same way and repeat 2 and 3 .

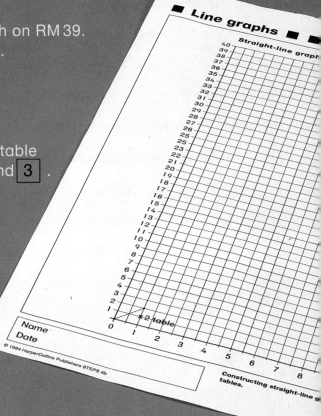

CHALLENGE

The blue point on the x2 table line
shows that $3\frac{1}{2} \times 2 = 7$.

■ Mark in **blue** the points which show:
   a $8\frac{1}{2} \times 2 = 17$
   b $5\frac{1}{2} \times 2 = 11$
   c $9\frac{1}{2} \times 2 = 19$.

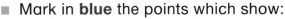

■ Mark in green the points which show:
   a $\frac{1}{2} \times 4 = 2$ b $8\frac{1}{2} \times 4 = 34$ c $9\frac{1}{2} \times 4 = 38$ d $5\frac{1}{2} \times 4 = 22$.

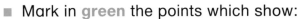

Digital sum patterns

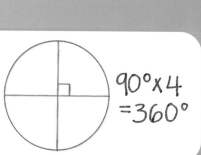

circular protractor

If you add the digits of a number, you can find its **digital sum**.

$10 \longrightarrow 1 + 0 = \mathbf{1}$

$68 \longrightarrow 6 + 8 = 14 \longrightarrow 1 + 4 = \mathbf{5}$

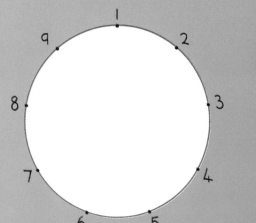

1   Draw round the circumference of your protractor.

2   Use your protractor to mark 9 evenly-spaced points on the circumference and number them.

3   Complete the digital sum pattern for the first 12 multiples in the x 2 table.

digital sum pattern (x 2 table)

2	→ 2
4	→ 4
6	→ 6
8	→ 8
10	→ 1
12	→
14	→
16	→
18	→
20	→
22	→
24	→

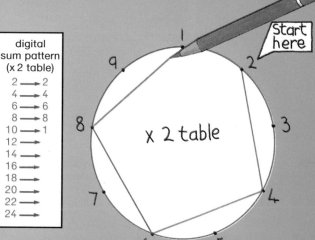

Start here

x 2 table

4   On your circle, join together in order points which match the digital sum pattern.

5   Repeat stages 1 to 4 for:

   a x 4 table   **b** x 7 table   **c** any other table.

6   Compare your results with others.

7   Explain why the x 2 and x 7 tables make the same pattern. Do other tables have the same pattern?

CHALLENGE

- Use your protractor to construct equal sectors of different angle sizes.
- Write what size of angles meet around the centre.

$90° \times 4 = 360°$

Circle patterns

1   To make this pattern:

- Set your compasses to a radius of 6 cm and draw a circle.

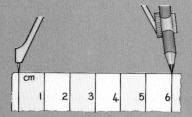

- Mark off the radius around the circumference 6 times.

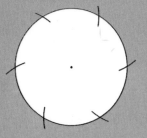

- Construct an arc about the marked centre.

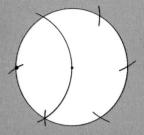

- Repeat this 5 more times, using each point on the circumference.

- You could colour your pattern.

2   Decide how to construct at least one of these patterns.

3   Design a similar pattern of your own.

Circles in use

compasses, RM D or 2 cm squared paper, scissors, glue

1   Try to construct one of these border patterns, using RM D or 2 cm squared paper. Colour your pattern.

2   Design a border pattern which includes circles or part-circles.

3   Ask your teacher if you can work in a group to do this.

Make a poster showing examples of circles in real life.

You might use drawings, cuttings from magazines, photographs or reference books from the library to help.

Include some of your favourite patterns too.

CHALLENGE

- Design a workcard for someone in another class to try out which will help them construct a circle pattern you like.

- Arrange for someone to try it out.

■ How likely? ■ ■ ■

Spinners

Pete, Rupa, Matt and Carrie have been colouring spinners in different ways.

For each spinner, they predict who will win the game.

> **Game**
> ■ Take turns to play.
> ■ If you spin the colour of your T-shirt, win a point.
> ■ First player with 5 points wins.

1 For this spinner predict:

   a Who is most likely to win?
   b Who is least likely to win?
   c Who has the better chance of winning than Matt?
   d For whom is it impossible to win?

2 Each player has made and coloured a hexagonal spinner.
From their descriptions, draw what you think each spinner looks like.

a Rupa and I have an equal chance of winning. It is impossible for Carrie or Matt to win.

b It is impossible for Pete to win. Carrie is most likely to win. Rupa has a poorer chance than Carrie. I am less likely to win than Rupa.

c Pete and I are unlikely to win. Matt and Rupa are more likely to win.

d Pete, Carrie and Matt have an equal chance of winning. But I am far more likely to win.

44

3   Design and colour a spinner of any shape
so that each player has an equal chance of winning.

4   Write rules for a game for 2 players
which uses a spinner like this.

Make the rules fair to each player.

5   Using the same spinner, write rules
for a game for 2 players so that one has
a **very poor chance** of winning.

6   Ask your teacher about trialling the fair
and unfair game.

Card chance

Imagine that these cards are face down in
random order in front of you, and you are
about to choose one.

7   Decide the best way to complete
these sentences about the cards.

a   I am certain to choose _____ .

b   It is impossible to choose numbers > _____ .

c   I am likely to choose a number > _____ .

< means fewer than
> means more than

d   I have a poor chance of choosing a number < _____ .

e   I have a better chance of choosing _____ than _____ .

f   I am equally likely to choose 7 or _____ .

■ Combinations ■ ■ ■ ■ ■ ■ ■

Ben packed 3 T-shirts and 2 pairs of shorts to wear on holiday.

If you had to show all the ways Ben could wear these, you might:

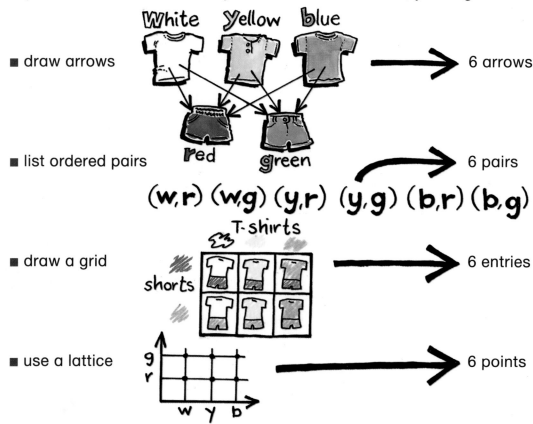

■ draw arrows → 6 arrows

■ list ordered pairs → 6 pairs

(w,r) (w,g) (y,r) (y,g) (b,r) (b,g)

■ draw a grid → 6 entries

■ use a lattice → 6 points

---

1   Caitlin packed 4 T-shirts and 3 pairs of shorts.
Find out all the ways she can wear these by:

     a   drawing arrows   **b**   listing ordered pairs
     c   drawing a grid   **d**   using a lattice.

2   Choose the method you think best
to show all the ways Caitlin could
choose from these options.

RULE: Each cone has only
one kind of ice cream.

raspberry   chocolate   vanilla

large   medium   small

STEPS 4b:15

3 Try to work out the answers to these in your head.

a How many pairs of socks if there are:

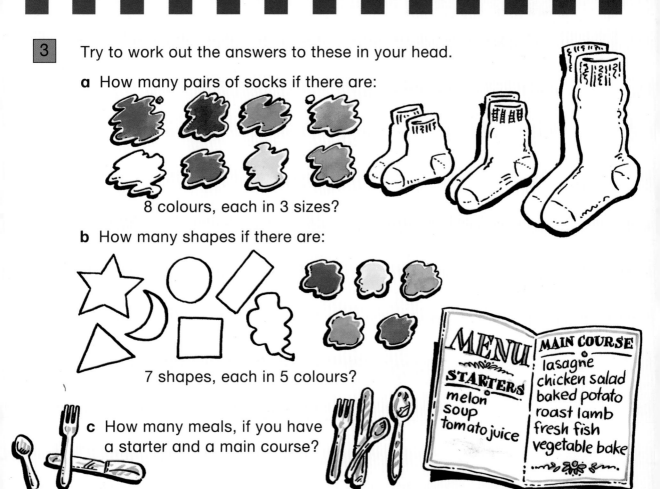

8 colours, each in 3 sizes?

b How many shapes if there are:

7 shapes, each in 5 colours?

c How many meals, if you have a starter and a main course?

MENU

STARTERS
melon
soup
tomato juice

MAIN COURSE
lasagne
chicken salad
baked potato
roast lamb
fresh fish
vegetable bake

4 Explain how you worked out the answers to **3** without drawing diagrams to help.

CHALLENGE

Design a lattice similar to this one for the set of shapes on the right.

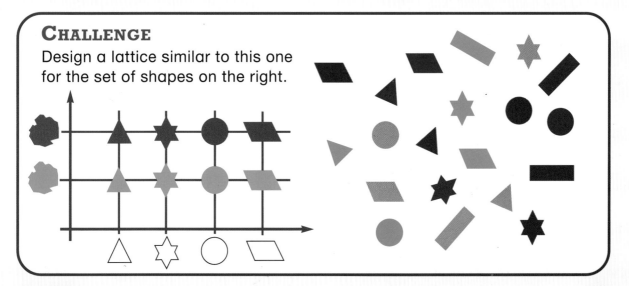

Likely totals

1 List all the totals you can get if you roll both dice and add the scores.

  is the same as

2 List the ways you can score each total.

For example, you can make a total of 4 like this.

Total of 4
1, 3
2, 2

3 Check that you have found 21 ways altogether in [2].

4 Complete these sentences.

If you total the scores on 2 dice in this way:

a You are most likely to get totals of _____ .
b You are least likely to get totals of _____ .
c It is impossible to get a total of less than _____ or more than _____ .
d You are certain to get a total between _____ and _____ .

5 Copy and complete this grid.
Then explain the link between this and the rest of your work.

Grouping and sharing

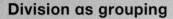

Division as grouping

Craig had 52 interlocking tiles. He gave 6 to as many people as he could so they could each make a net for a cube.

Division as sharing

Georgia shared 52 cards between 6 people to play a game.

1 Copy and complete.

   a ■ ___ people got 6 tiles and ___ tiles were left over.
     ■ 52 will make ___ groups of ___ and ___ remaining.
     ■ 52 ÷ 6 =

   b ■ ___ people got ___ cards each and ___ were left over.
     ■ 52 shared between 6 will make ___ each and ___ remaining.
     ■ 52 ÷ 6 =

2 a Write a grouping story for one of these.
   b Write a sharing story for another of these.

47 ÷ 6   54 ÷ 7   61 ÷ 9

35 ÷ 8

3 Show how you find the answers to these.

   a I started with 60 plants.
     I planted 8 in every tub.
     I had 4 plants left over.
     How many tubs did I fill?

   b I bought some tickets at £7 each.
     I got £1 change from £50.
     How many tickets did I buy?

   c I shared a bag of 48 jelly beans
     between my 4 friends and myself.
     How many each?
     How many were left over?

CHALLENGE

■ If I buy some audio tapes at £5 each and some video tapes at £7 each, and I spend £100, how many of each do I buy?

■ Find more than one possibility.

Answers for colours

1 Replace each ⬤ with one of these numbers: ⑤ ② ❾ ⑥

   a 23 ÷ 4 = ⬤ remainder 3   **b** 19 ÷ ⬤ = ⬤ remainder 1

   c 89 ÷ ⬤ = ⬤ remainder 8   **d** 48 ÷ 7 = ⬤ remainder ⬤

   e 26 ÷ 4 = ⬤ remainder ⬤   **f** 59 ÷ ⬤ = ⬤ remainder ⬤

2 Divide one **blue** number
by one **red** number each time.
Find all the possible answers.

                                  4 43
                        5 31   6 26
                                7 37

3 Make the given number of answers.

> **RULE:** ▬ is a 2-digit number.
> ■ is a 1-digit number.

   a ▬ ÷ ■ = 3 remainder 7   **2 correct answers**

   b ▬ ÷ ■ = 8 remainder 5   **4 correct answers**

   c ▬ ÷ ■ = 5 remainder 4   **5 correct answers**

   d ▬ ÷ ■ = 2 remainder 3   **6 correct answers**

Write two diffferent answers each time.

4
> **RULE:** Replace ■ with a 1-digit number.

   a 10 ÷ ■ = ■ remainder 0   **b** 13 ÷ ■ = ■ remainder 1

   c 22 ÷ ■ = ■ remainder 2   **d** 35 ÷ ■ = ■ remainder 3

   e 49 ÷ ■ = ■ remainder 4   **f** 50 ÷ ■ = ■ remainder 2

   g 62 ÷ ■ = ■ remainder 6   **h** 79 ÷ ■ = ■ remainder 7

CHALLENGE

Make up more examples like those in **4** for a friend to try.

Stick shapes

Jade, Donald and Lucy had to work out
how many triangles they could make with 74 sticks.

Jade wrote: Donald wrote: Lucy wrote:

$$\begin{array}{r} 74 \\ -60 \\ \hline 14 \\ -12 \\ \hline 2 \end{array} \begin{array}{l} (20\triangle s) \\ \\ (4\triangle s) \end{array}$$

24 triangles and
2 sticks left.

$$3\overline{)74} \quad \text{24 triangles}$$
$$-30 \ (10\triangle s)$$
$$\overline{44}$$
$$-30 \ (10\triangle s)$$
$$\overline{14}$$
$$-12 \ (4\triangle s)$$
$$\overline{2} \ \text{sticks left}$$

$$3\overline{)74} \quad \text{24 r2}$$

24 triangles and
2 sticks left.

Choose the way **you** like to work these out.

1 How many **crosses** could you make
from these numbers of sticks?

  a 53   **b** 83   **c** 97   **d** 68

2 How many **triangles** could you make from the same numbers of sticks?

3 How many **squares** could you make from the same numbers of sticks?

4 How many of these shapes can you make if you start with **99** each time?

a

pentagon

b

hexagon

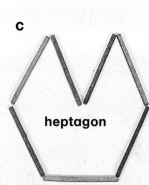

c

heptagon

d

octagon

CHALLENGE   **RULE:** is a 2-digit number.

Show that you can find 13 ways to complete this: ● ÷ 7 = ● rem 6.

Rod division

Here are the Cuisenaire rods with their lengths.

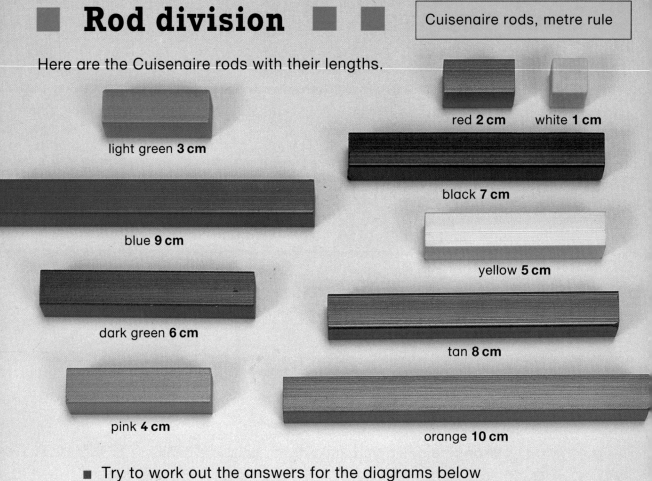

light green **3 cm**

red **2 cm**   white **1 cm**

black **7 cm**

blue **9 cm**

yellow **5 cm**

dark green **6 cm**

tan **8 cm**

pink **4 cm**

orange **10 cm**

- Try to work out the answers for the diagrams below without using rods or a rule.
- Show any workings-out.
- **Afterwards**, check with rods and a rule, if you want.

1   Copy and complete this arrow diagram.

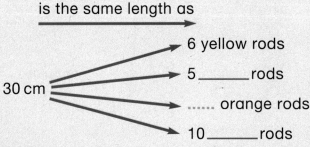

is the same length as

30 cm
- 6 yellow rods
- 5 _____ rods
- ...... orange rods
- 10 _____ rods

2   Draw arrow diagrams in the same way for these.

a	12 cm	b	56 cm
c	40 cm	d	18 cm
e	54 cm	f	20 cm
g	36 cm	h	16 cm

RULES
- Draw 2, 3 or 4 arrows each time.
- Use only 1 colour of rod for each arrow.
- Use up to 10 rods.

52

3 In each of these examples the rods, fitted end to end, will equal **1 metre**. Find the missing number or colour in each set.

a 8 tan and ...... blue rods.

b 8 yellow rods and ...... dark green rods.

c 10 black rods and 10 _____ rods.

d 8 _____ rods and 5 pink rods.

e ...... blue and 7 pink rods.

f 6 _____ rods and 7 orange rods.

g 7 black, 7 light green and 6 _____ rods.

h ...... pink, 10 yellow and 7 red rods.

4 Decide the best way to find the missing numbers or colours.

a ...... black rods and 1 light green rod equal 59 cm.

b 9 _____ rods and 1 red rod equal 38 cm.

c ...... dark green rods and 1 blue rod equal 57 cm.

d 6 tan rods and 1 _____ rod equal 58 cm.

e ...... blue rods and 1 white rod equal 46 cm.

f ...... orange rods and 1 tan rod equal 88 cm.

g ...... yellow rods, 7 pink rods and 1 red rod equal 80 cm.

CHALLENGE

Some light green rods, some yellow rods and one orange rod measure 85 cm long when fitted end to end.

■ How many light green rods and how many yellow rods are there?
■ Try to find more than one correct answer.

Exploring volume ■ ■ ■

A Centicube has a volume of **1 cubic centimetre**.
One way to write this is **1 cu cm**.

1

a Use the cubes to make this red shape.

b Fit a blue shape on top of the red shape.

c Fit a green shape on top like this:

2 Add the fewest possible white cubes to make a **cuboid**.

3 Write the volume of:

   a the white cubes   **b** the 'not white' cubes   **c** the whole cuboid.

4 Add the fewest possible yellow cubes to make a **cube**.

5 Write the volume of:

   a the yellow cubes   **b** the 'not yellow' cubes   **c** the whole cube.

6 Build a tower on top of this shape.

Use 27 cubes.
Write: There are ___ cu cm in the base.
There are ___ layers.
The **volume** is ___ cu cm.

7 Use the 27 cubes to build a larger **cube**.
Write: There are ___ cu cm in the base.
There are ___ layers.
The **volume** is ___ cu cm.

CHALLENGE

- Make these 8 shapes.
- Fit them all together to make a cube.
- What is its volume?

54

Sliced cuboids

Another short way to write cubic centimetres is cm³.
Use this way when you do this page.

There are 4 equal slices.

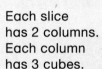

Each slice
has 2 columns.
Each column
has 3 cubes.

This cuboid is made
from 24 cubes.

**The volume of
the whole cuboid** = number of cm³ in each slice × the number of slices

= 6 cm³ × 4

= **24 cm³**

a

b

| 1 | ■ Find the volume
of these cuboids. |

■ Two are shown
sliced to help you.

■ Record in the same way
as the red type above.

■ Use cubes if it helps.

c

d

e

Working out volumes

This cuboid is made from Centicubes.

4 slices (length 4 cm)
2 columns (width 2 cm)
3 cubes in each column (height 3 cm)

Volume = 4 × 2 × 3 cm³
       = 24 cm³

1 Copy and complete **a** and **b** in the same way as above.

a — slices (length in cm)
   — columns (width in cm)
   — cubes in each column (height in cm)

Volume = — × — × — cm³
       = — cm³

b — (length in cm)
   — (width in cm)
   — (height in cm)

Volume = — × — × — cm³
       = — cm³

2 Copy and complete:

Volume in cm³ = _____ in cm × _____ in cm × _____ in cm.

3 Show how you find the volume of these cuboids
made from centimetre cubes.
(Use cubes to make them if it helps.)

a

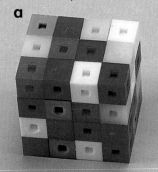

b

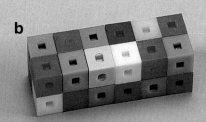

c

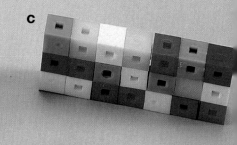

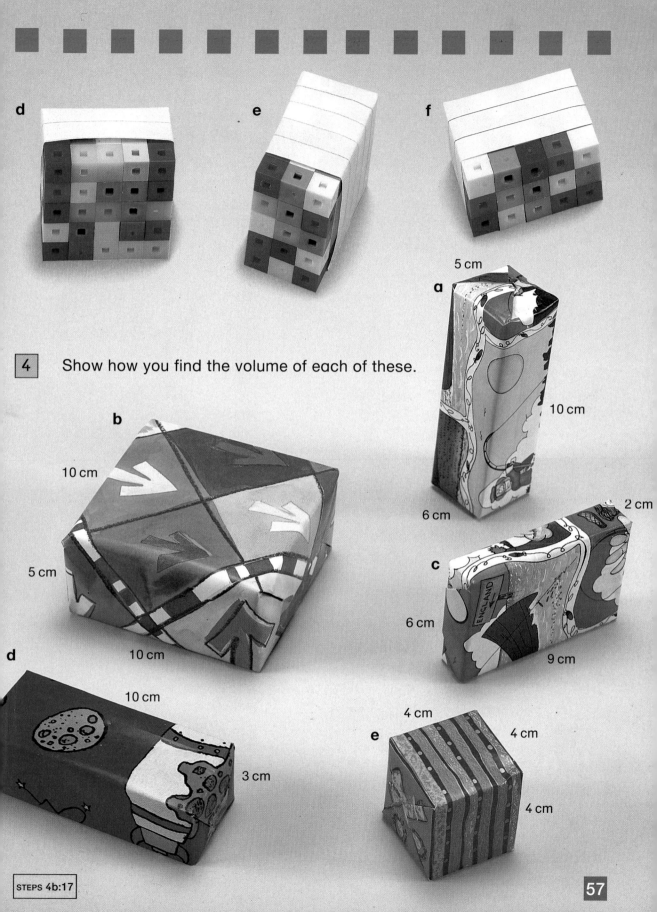

d

e

f

4 Show how you find the volume of each of these.

a

5 cm

10 cm

6 cm

b

10 cm

5 cm

10 cm

c

2 cm

6 cm

9 cm

d

10 cm

3 cm

e

4 cm

4 cm

4 cm

Fractions of sets

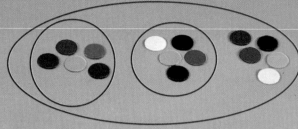

Use cubes or counters to help you
with this page if you want.
Show all your working-out.

1 This is one way to
show $\frac{2}{3}$ of a set.

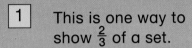

$\frac{2}{3}$ of 15 counters = 10 counters

2 Draw two other diagrams to show $\frac{2}{3}$ of a set.
Start with a different number of objects each time.

3 For each of these fractions draw two diagrams.
Start with a different number of objects each time.

   a $\frac{3}{4}$ of a set   **b** $\frac{5}{6}$ of a set   **c** $\frac{3}{8}$ of a set

4 Decide the best way to find the answers to these.

  a Jason used $\frac{1}{4}$ of his £28 savings to
buy a cassette. Then he used $\frac{2}{3}$ of the
money left to buy a camera.
How much did he spend?

  b $\frac{5}{6}$ of 36 apples in a box are green; the
rest are red. **How many of each colour?**

  d 9 squares of chocolate
have been eaten,
which is $\frac{1}{4}$ of the whole bar.
How many squares are left?

  c There were 40 Smarties in the tube,
$\frac{2}{5}$ were eaten. **How many are left?**

CHALLENGE

- Use numbers up to 100.
- Show that you can complete this in 12 ways: $\frac{3}{8}$ of ___ = ___ .
- Show that you can complete this in 16 ways: $\frac{5}{6}$ of ___ = ___ .

Top-heavy fractions

The same amount of pizza is on each tray.

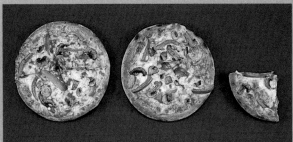 

1 whole + 1 whole + 1 quarter

$= 1 + 1 + \frac{1}{4}$

$= 2 + \frac{1}{4}$

$= 2\frac{1}{4}$

$2\frac{1}{4}$ is called a mixed number.

4 quarters + 4 quarters + 1 quarter

$= \frac{4}{4} + \frac{4}{4} + \frac{1}{4}$

= 9 quarters

$= \frac{9}{4}$

$\frac{9}{4}$ is called a top-heavy fraction.

1   Write the amount coloured as:

■ a mixed number   ■ a top-heavy fraction.

a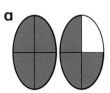

b

c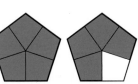

d

e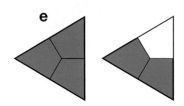

f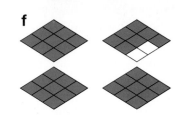

2   Choose the best way to show these amounts in pictures.

   a $1\frac{7}{10}$ **b** $\frac{19}{8}$ **c** $\frac{24}{5}$ **d** $2\frac{3}{4}$ **e** $4\frac{2}{3}$

CHALLENGE

Write about this in
5 different ways. Show as:

■ mixed numbers
■ top-heavy fractions.

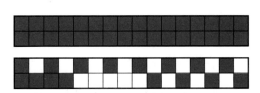

People fractions

Check that you can find 36 people in the park.

1   Write how many people are:

    a wearing glasses   **b** carrying handbags   **c** wearing hats
    d walking dogs   **e** eating ice-cream.

2   Compare your answers with a neighbour.

3   For your answer to 1 **a** you can draw a diagram like this:

    is the same as

    6 out of 36 ←→ 1 out of 6

    $\frac{1}{6}$

    Draw a similar diagram for 1 **b**, **c**, **d** and **e**.

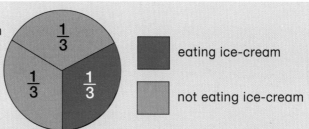

The three sectors in this fraction pie chart show that:

$\frac{1}{3}$ are eating ice-cream

$\frac{2}{3}$ are not eating ice-cream.

■ eating ice-cream

□ not eating ice-cream

4 Using a circular protractor, divide up circles in the same way to show how many are and are not:

a wearing hats **b** wearing glasses
c walking dogs **d** carrying handbags.

5 Construct fraction pie-charts like the one shown above for this data.

a There are 28 children in the class. 7 play the recorder.

b 5 out of 30 children in the class play tennis.

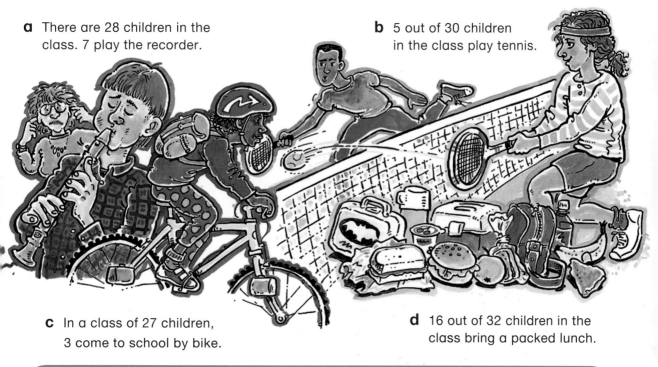

c In a class of 27 children, 3 come to school by bike.

d 16 out of 32 children in the class bring a packed lunch.

CHALLENGE

On one pie chart, show the fraction of each colour in this set of counters.

Shape F on RM 47 has been made by plotting points (7,7) (10,7) (7,11) (7,7) and joining them in order.

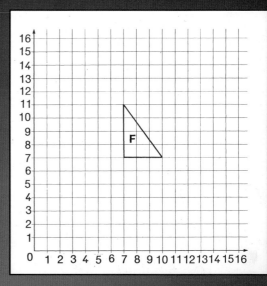

1 **a** Put the co-ordinates of F through this function machine to give you the co-ordinates for shape **G**.

Shape F
(7,7) (10,7) (7,11) (7,7) ➡ Add 5 to the **first** number in each co-ordinate. ➡ Shape G
(,) (,) (,) (,)

b Plot the points for shape G on RM 48 and join them in order.
This function machine is a Move East machine.

2 Do the same for these machines.

a Shape F
(7,7) (10,7) (7,11) (7,7) ➡ Subtract 6 from the **first** number in each co-ordinate. ➡ Shape H
(,) (,) (,) (,)

b Shape F
(7,7) (10,7) (7,11) (7,7) ➡ Add 4 to the **second** number in each co-ordinate. ➡ Shape I
(,) (,) (,) (,)

c Shape F
(7,7) (10,7) (7,11) (7,7) ➡ Subtract 5 from the **second** number in each co-ordinate. ➡ Shape J
(,) (,) (,) (,)

3 For each machine in **2** write a sentence like the one in orange.

4 **a** Put the co-ordinates of shape F through this 2-operation machine to give you the co-ordinates for shape K.

Shape F
(7,7) (10,7) (7,11) (7,7)

Shape K
(,) (,) (,) (,)

Add 4 to the **first** number in each co-ordinate.

(,)(,)(,) (,)

Add 4 to the **second** number in each co-ordinate.

b Plot the points for shape K on RM 48 and join them in order.
c Copy and complete: This is a **Move ..... - ..... machine.**

5 Repeat **4** a–c to make shape L.

Shape F
(7,7) (10,7) (7,11) (7,7)

Shape L
(,) (,) (,) (,)

Add 6 to the **first** number in each co-ordinate.

(,)(,)(,) (,)

Subtract 6 from the **second** number in each co-ordinate.

CHALLENGE

■ Design 2-operation machines which will translate shape F to these positions.

Translate means slide or move in a straight line.

a
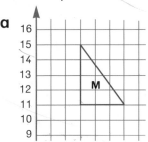

b
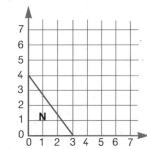

■ Copy and complete: **a** is a **Move**____ -____ machine and
b is a **Move**____ -____ machine.

Co-ordinates translation

Shape **A** has been made
by plotting the points
(1,1) (4,1) (3,4) (1,4) (1,1)
and joining them in order.

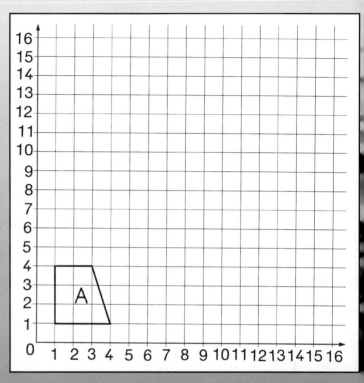

1   Copy shape **A** onto RM 47.

2

   a Add 5 to each of the **first**
     numbers in **A**'s
     co-ordinates.
     Copy and complete
     this pattern:
     (6,1) (,1) (,4) (,4) (,1).

   b Plot these points in order
     on RM 47 to make
     shape **B**.

   c Complete this sentence in your book:
     Shape A has been translated____squares to the____to make shape B.

3   **a** Add 5 to the **first** numbers in **B**'s co-ordinates.
     Copy and complete this pattern: (11,1) (,1) (,4) (,4) (,1).
     Plot these points and join them in order to make shape **C**.

   b How far and in which direction has shape **A** been translated
     to make shape **C**?

4   Add 4 to the **second** numbers in **C**'s co-ordinates.
   Copy and complete: (11,5) (,) (,) (,) (,).
   Plot these points and join them in order to make shape **D**.

5   Add 6 to the **second** numbers in **D**'s co-ordinates.
   Copy and complete: (11,11) (,) (,) (,) (,).
   Plot these points and join them in order to make shape **E**.

6   Explain how you could translate shape **A** to shape **E** in one move.

Standard weights

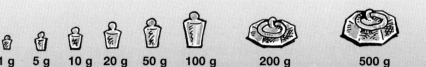

1 g	5 g	10 g	20 g	50 g	100 g	200 g	500 g	1 kg

1 Work out the **fewest** standard weights you could add to the left pan to make it balance the right one.

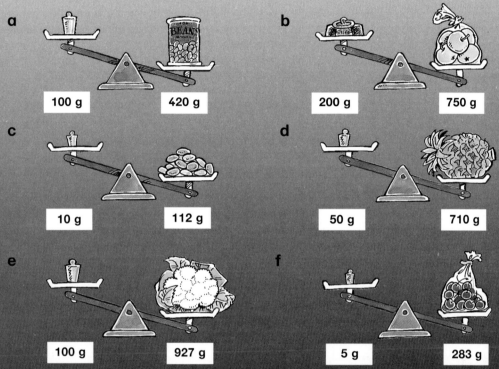

a
| 100 g | 420 g |

b
| 200 g | 750 g |

c
| 10 g | 112 g |

d
| 50 g | 710 g |

e
| 100 g | 927 g |

f
| 5 g | 283 g |

2 Work out the weight of each object.

	Standard weights used					
Object	**1 kg**	**500 g**	**100 g**	**50 g**	**20 g**	**10 g**
a Bucket	–	–	1	2	6	4
b Brick	1	–	–	1	4	–
c Shoe	–	–	–	1	5	3
d Chair	3	1	2	4	1	5

CHALLENGE

If and , how many marbles will balance the apple?

Approximating

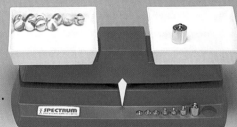

Work with one or two friends if you can.

1
- Place a 50 g weight on one pan.
- Place marbles on the second pan until the pans balance.
- Write about how many marbles weigh 50 g.

2 Without doing any more weighing, write:

a About how many marbles will balance 200 g.
b About how many will balance a half-kilogram.
c About how many will balance a kilogram.
d How much 1 marble weighs, to the nearest gram.

Use a calculator to find answers if it helps.

3 On the scales, find the weight of 20 marbles.

4 Without doing any more weighing, write the approximate weight of:

a 100 marbles   b 10 marbles   c 5 marbles
d 50 marbles   e 200 marbles   f 1 marble.

5 Compare your answers to **2** d and **4** f.
If your answers are not the same, try to explain why.

CHALLENGE
Find small objects such as:

beans   drawing pins   paper clips   grains

- Without weighing them all, find about how many of each will balance 1 kg.
- Show how you work out the answers.
- Record your answers like this.

About ... paper clips →
About ... grains → will balance 1 kg.
About ... beans →

Gross and net weights

scales, containers, dried peas

The weight of a container and its contents together is called the **gross weight**.

The weight of the contents alone is called the **net weight**.

The net weight is the gross weight minus the weight of the container.

1 Choose a box or container.

    a Find and record its weight in grams.
    b Fill it with dried peas.
    c Find and record the **gross weight** of the box and peas.
    d Calculate the **net weight** of the peas.

2   **a** Copy this table.
    b Read the scale below and record the **gross weight** of each of the foods.
    c Complete the table.

Weight (grams)	A	B	C	D	E	F
Gross weight						
Net weight	11g	170g	100g			
Empty container				330g	195g	380g

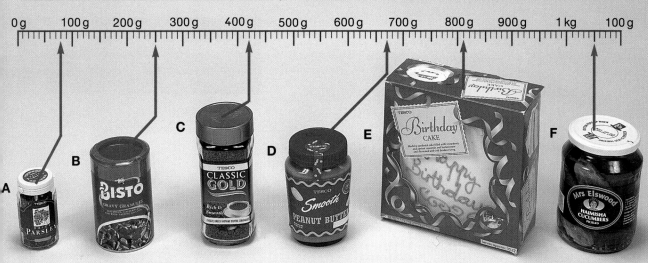

Median and mode

| 140 cm | 133 cm | 140 cm | 146 cm | 122 cm | 128 cm | 135 cm |
| Hayley | Nasreen | James | Bobby | Joanne | Harry | Pritam |

1 List these heights in order.
What is the height of the child
in the middle of your list?

> The height of the child in the middle
> is called the **median** height.

2 List these hands in order of area.

| 91 cm² | 105 cm² | 100 cm² | 94 cm² | 89 cm² | 100 cm² | 98 cm² |
| Harry | Hayley | Bobby | Pritam | Joanne | Nasreen | James |

3 Write the **median** area of the hands.

> When there is an even number of
> measurements, the median is
> **half-way between the two
> middle numbers**.

4 Paul joins the group.
He is 131 cm tall.

  a Write a new list of heights in order.
  b Write the new median height.

5   **a** Include Paul's hand in a new ordered list
     of the hands' areas.
  b Write the new median area of the hands.

93 cm²
Paul

6 Find the height which
occurs most often in 1 .

> The measure which occurs most
> often is called the **mode**.

7 Write the area which is the **mode** in 2 .

68

These tables show the shoe sizes of Paul's class.

Red Group	
Clare	1
Joseph	$4\frac{1}{2}$
Lauren	6
Steven	3
Rajinder	$3\frac{1}{2}$
Harry	$4\frac{1}{2}$
Ellis	2
Ross	4
Joanne	$1\frac{1}{2}$
Nasreen	$2\frac{1}{2}$

Green Group	
Mira	$3\frac{1}{2}$
Ricky	2
Julian	$4\frac{1}{2}$
Gemma	5
Camilla	$5\frac{1}{2}$
Diego	$4\frac{1}{2}$
Melody	$4\frac{1}{2}$
James	$6\frac{1}{2}$
Jafar	$3\frac{1}{2}$
Nicole	4

Blue Group	
Michael	$6\frac{1}{2}$
Hattie	$4\frac{1}{2}$
Paul	5
Tarun	4
Lisa	3
Bobby	7
Hayley	$5\frac{1}{2}$
Pritam	5
Ben	4
Katy	$4\frac{1}{2}$

8 Copy and complete this table for the shoe sizes.

shoe size	1	$1\frac{1}{2}$	2	$2\frac{1}{2}$	3	$3\frac{1}{2}$	4	$4\frac{1}{2}$	5	$5\frac{1}{2}$	6	$6\frac{1}{2}$	7
number of children													

9 For the shoe sizes, write:

    a the median   **b** the mode.

10 Write the **range** of the shoe sizes.

> The **range** is the difference between the largest and the smallest size.

11 Explain why a shoe manufacturer finds it useful to know the most common shoe size (the mode) for women.

CHALLENGE

■ Find 5 shoe sizes for which the median is size 4 and the mode is size 3.
■ Find different ways to do it.

Mean and range

The mean is an amount which represents a whole set of amounts. It is calculated like this:

- Add together the amounts:
  £8 + £6 + £2 + £5 + £4 = £25.

- Count up the number of amounts: 5.

- Divide the total by the number of amounts:
  £25 ÷ 5 = £5.
  The mean is £5.

- The **range** is the **difference** between the largest and smallest amounts in the set:
  £8 – £2 = £6.
  The range is £6.

Sometimes we use the word 'average' instead of mean.

---

1 Write the value of one coin or note which is the mean of these.

a

b

c

d

e

f

---

2 You could buy 4 stickers at 20p each with the coins in **1 a**.
Write similar sentences for examples **1 b** to **f**.

3 Calculate the mean and range of these prices.

a Jackets   **b** Chocolate   **c** Ices

d Books and tapes   **e** Personal stereos

4 Buying 2 jackets at £25 and £39 costs the same as buying 2 jackets at £32 each.

Write a similar sentence for examples **3** **b** to **e**.

CHALLENGE

- Use a set of cards numbered from £1 to £20.
- Investigate sets of 3 cards with ranges of £5, £6 or £7.
- Investigate sets of cards with means of £8, £9 or £10.

Posting packages

This table shows the cost
of posting letters and packages
(in 1994).

Weight not over	First Class	Second Class	Weight not over	First Class	Second Class
60 g	25p	19p	500 g	£1.25p	98p
100 g	38p	29p	600 g	£1.55p	£1.20p
150 g	47p	36p	700 g	£1.90p	£1.20p
200 g	57p	43p	750 g	£2.05p	£1.45p
250 g	67p	52p	800 g	£2.15p	Not admissible over 750 g
300 g	77p	61p	900 g	£2.35p	
350 g	88p	70p	1000 g	£2.50p	
400 g	£1.00	79p		Each extra 250 g, or part thereof, 65p	
450 g	£1.13	89p			

1 Write the cost of posting each
of these packages **first class**.

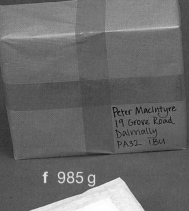

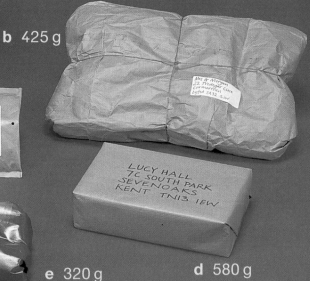

b 425 g

c 270 g

f 985 g

a 45 g

e 320 g

d 580 g

2 Write which stamps you would use on each package.
The stamps are shown opposite.
Use **as few as possible** each time.

3 How much change would you get for the stamps for
the same packages if you used these to pay for them?

a

b

c

d

e

f

4   Write the cost of posting each of these packages **second class**.

     a 80 g   **b** 310 g   **c** 675 g   **d** 445 g   **e** 490 g   **f** 180 g

5   Write which stamps you would use on each package.
     Choose as few as possible each time.

6   How much change would you get for the stamps for
     the same packages if you used these to pay for them?

a   **b**    **c**

d   **e**    **f**

CHALLENGE

- Explain why this package costs £3·15 to send.
- Draw more packages between 1 kg and 3 kg in weight.
- Write the cost of posting each one.

1160 g

Spending a gift token

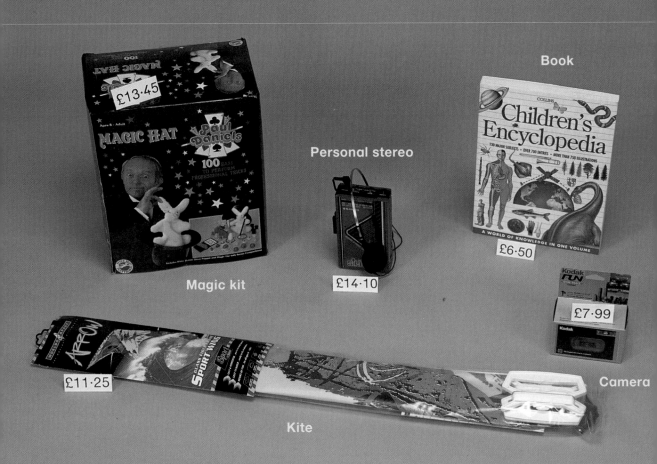

Book

Personal stereo

£13·45

MAGIC HAT

Magic kit

£14·10

Children's Encyclopedia

£6·50

£7·99

Camera

£11·25

Kite

Ross was given a £20 gift token.
He has found 10 things he wants to buy. He has to choose 2 of them.

1 List 5 different pairs of things he could buy
   and the total cost of each pair.
   Each pair must cost more than £17.

2 Work out the change he would
   get from each pair. You could
   use a table like this:

pair	total cost	change from £20

CHALLENGE

Show how you could buy two things for exactly:

a £14·95   **b** £16·24   **c** £23·60   **d** £26·60.

Game

£12·50

Watch

£9·50

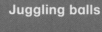
Juggling balls

£5·75

Snorkel

£4·99

Mask

£8·45

The store reduces
its prices in a sale.

SALE

PRICES SLASHED!

TWO WEEKS ONLY

All items...

... up to £5 reduced by £1·25!

... between £5 and £10 reduced by £2·50!!

... more than £10 reduced by £4·50!!!

3   Work out the sale price
of each item and list them, cheapest first.

CHALLENGE

Show how you could buy two things in the sale for exactly:

a £16·60   **b** £12·95   **c** £10·00   **d** £9·69.

Right-angled triangles

REMEMBER: This square has an area of **one square centimetre**.
We can write this as **1 sq cm** or **1 cm²**.

1 Work out the area of the shapes enclosed in the red lines.

Look for clues to help you

a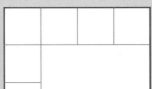

b

c

d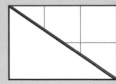

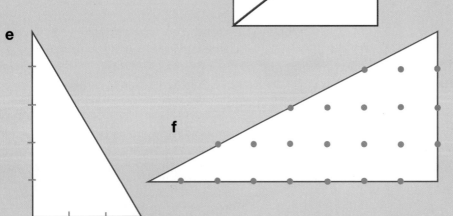

CHALLENGE

On RM A, draw pairs of right-angled triangles with the same area.

RULE: The sides of each pair must be different lengths.

Areas of parallelograms

A parallelogram is a quadrilateral with opposite sides parallel.

One way to find the area of a parallelogram is to change it into a rectangle.

1 Draw and cut out 2 congruent parallelograms like this from RM A.

2 Cut a right-angled triangle from the end of one of the parallelograms.

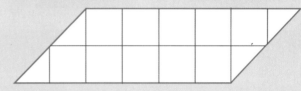

3 Change the parallelogram into a rectangle by sliding the triangle to the other side.

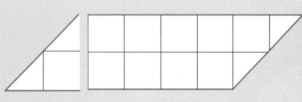

4 Glue both shapes in your book like this. Copy and complete the sentence.

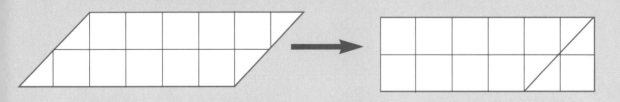

The area of the parallelogram and the rectangle is .... cm^2 (.......sq cm).

5 Cut out more pairs of congruent parallelograms. Repeat 2 to 4 for each pair.

Tangrams

RM 56 and A, scissors, glue

A tangram is a square cut into 7 shapes which are used to create new shapes. We think they were first used in China thousands of years ago.

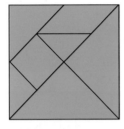 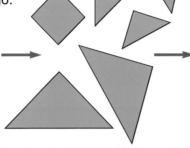 

1 Cut up one of the tangrams on RM 56.
Use it to make a copy of **one** of these pictures.
Glue the pieces down on a backing sheet.

Bird

Cat

Kicking

2
- Cut up a second tangram.
- Design your own picture or pattern.
- Use all the pieces. Don't overlap them.
- Give it a title.
- Decorate it like the one shown if you want.

3 Cut up a third tangram and jumble up the pieces.
Try to fit them back together again to make
the square without copying from another tangram.

4 Copy and complete this:
... sq cm (... cm²) will fit on the tangram's surface because ...

5
- Use the 7 pieces to make 2 matching squares.
- Use the pieces shown in **green** for one and the pieces shown in **yellow** for another.
- Glue the squares down.

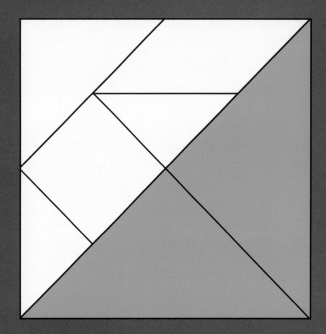

6   Copy and complete:

The area of each square is ... sq cm (... cm²) because ... .

7   Cut up the last tangram.
Use the two tangram pieces shown above in green to make a:

a right-angled triangle   **b** parallelogram
c pentagon   **d** hexagon.

Draw each shape as you make it. Show the 2 pieces.

8   Now copy and complete this:

The area of each shape in 7 is ... sq cm (... cm²) because ... .

CHALLENGE

- On RM A, design a tangram with sides 12 cm long.
- Number the pieces as shown.
- Decide the best way to find the area of each piece.
- Show all your workings-out.

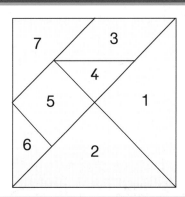

Rotating stars

compasses, 10 cm circular protractor, tracing paper

1

a

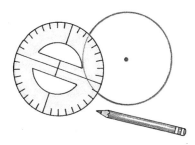

Mark a pencil point on your paper. Draw lightly in pencil around the outline of a circular protractor centred on the point.

b

Divide the circumference into 4 equal parts.

c

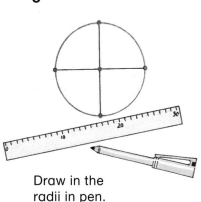

Draw in the radii in pen.

d

Use the compasses to draw lightly a smaller circle inside the first one.

e

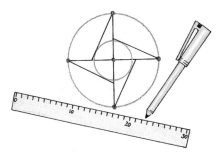

Draw pen lines to connect points on the outer circle to the inner circle.

f

Rub out the circles and colour your star if you want.

2 Complete. **This star has rotational symmetry of order** ... .

3 To check that you are correct:

- Mark a small cross near the star.
- Trace the star and cross.
- Line up the centres and rotate the tracing.
- Count how often it fits in one whole turn.

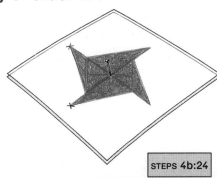

STEPS 4b:24

4 Design a star with rotational symmetry of order **6** in the same way.

5 Make other stars starting in the same way. Add extra decoration to show off their symmetry if you want.
Repeat **2** and **3** for each star you make.

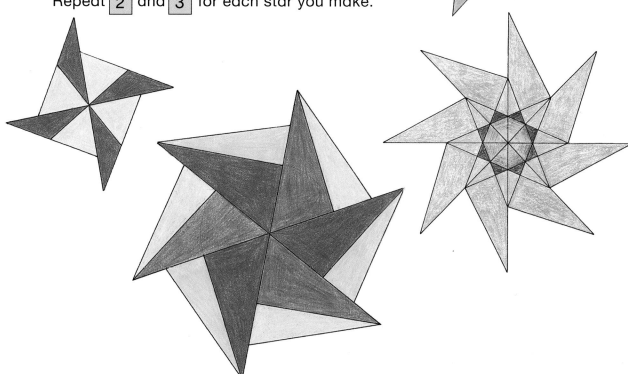

CHALLENGE

Design different patterns
with an area of 12 square centimetres
and rotational symmetry of order 2 or 4.

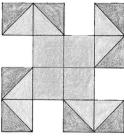

order 4

This pattern was designed
on grid **A** on RM 57 ...

... then it was coloured to show
its rotational symmetry of order 6.

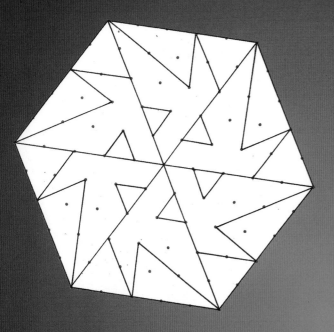

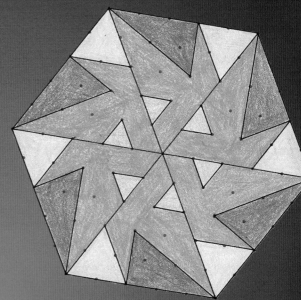

1   On grid **A**, design your own pattern with
rotational symmetry of order 6.

CHALLENGE

This pattern was designed
on grid **B** of RM 57
using compasses.

It has rotational symmetry
of order 4.

- On grid **B**, design your own
  pattern with compasses so
  that it has rotational
  symmetry of order 4.

Million puzzlers   calculator

Work with one or two friends.
Find the best way to work out the answers
to as many of these as you can.

1 How far away from home
would 1 000 000 strides take you?

2 If you fitted together 1 000 000
Centicubes to make a larger cube,
what would its measurements be?

3 If you had a fortnight's holiday,
would your holiday be longer
or shorter than a million seconds?

4 If an elephant has been alive for 1 000 000 hours,
what age will it be?

...mathematics...

5 Work out how long
you think it would take you
to say 'mathematics' one million times.

6 If you stacked a million
2p coins, how high
would the
stack be?

7 What weight would balance
a million 1p coins?
How much are
the coins worth?

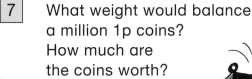

8 Would your classroom
hold a million
builders' bricks?

9 In a million days time,
we will be closer
to the year 3000
than 2000.
True or false?

Millions and millions!

millions	hundreds of thousands	tens of thousands	thousands	hundreds	tens	units

Use a 7-spike abacus to help you when you need it.

When we write large numbers, we usually use commas and not spaces:
1,000,000

1 Use RM 60 to show numbers **a** to **f**, like this, on the abacus diagram and place value boards.
Then write them in figures.

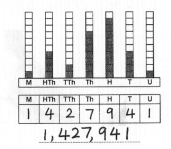

M	HTh	TTh	Th	H	T	U
1	4	2	7	9	4	1

1,427,941

a One million, three hundred and fifty-four thousand, eight hundred and two.
b One million, thirteen thousand and twelve.
c One million, two hundred and two thousand and four.
d One million and one.
e One million, ninety thousand, five hundred and seven.
f One million, one hundred thousand, eight hundred and twenty-three.

2 Choose 4 numbers between 1 000 000 and 1 999 999.
Write about each one in this way.

1 206 315 ⟷ one million, two hundred and six thousand, three hundred and fifteen.

3 1 742 653 The 4 is in the ten thousands place.
The 4 is worth 40 000.

Write about the **red** digit in each of these in the same way.

a 1 264 583   b 1 327 496   c 1 682 457
d 1 597 345   e 1 111 210   f 1 987 342

4 Record on a 7-spike abacus and in figures **ten** numbers you can make.

RULES:
- You can only put beads on the three left-hand spikes.
- You can only use 5 beads.

Example:

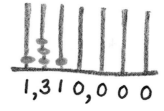

1,310,000

5 Write these digits on small squares of paper. Arrange them to make what you think is:

1 2 6 4 0 5 3

a the smallest odd number over a million
b the number nearest to one million
c the largest even number between one and two million.

> Write your answers in your book.

6
- Use the squares from **5**.
- Show that you can put the 2 in six other positions in a frame like this:
- Draw the frames.
- Write the value of the 2 each time.

M	H Th	T Th	Th	H	T	U
3	6	1	4	2	0	5

↓
100 x 2

CHALLENGE
- Fit these 4 loose spikes on the abacus in different ways to find **twelve** 6-digit **even** numbers.
- Draw each abacus and write the number it shows.

Roman numerals

Long ago, the Romans did not have a place value system.
Instead they wrote capital letters side by side
to stand for numerals. They used:

1 = **I**	6 = **VI**
2 = **II**	7 = **VII**
3 = **III**	8 = **VIII**
4 = **IV**	9 = **IX**
5 = **V**	10 = **X**

I for 1   **V** for 5   **X** for 10   **L** for 50
C for 100   **D** for 500   **M** for 1000

Their system works like this:

- If a letter for a smaller numeral is written to the **left**
  of a letter for a larger numeral, you **subtract**.
  IV means 5 – 1 = 4.
  XC means 100 – 10 = 90.

- If a symbol for a smaller numeral is written to the **right**
  of a letter for a larger numeral, you **add**.
  VIII means 5 + 3 = 8.
  MCD means 1000 + (500-100) = 1400.

- You never use more than three of the same letters
  next to each other.
  (Clockmakers sometimes break this rule and write **IIII** for 4.)

- Where have you seen Roman numerals used?

1   Work out what numbers these numerals represent.

     a XXIII   **b XLVI**   **c CD**   **d XLIX**   **e MXC**

2   Write these in Roman numerals.

     a 83   **b** 39   **c** 248   **d** 1250   **e** 999

3   Choose some more numbers and write them as Roman numerals.

> ### CHALLENGE
>
> Write some multiplication tables
> in Roman numerals.
>
> II × I = II
> II × II = IV
> II × III = VI ...

STEPS 4b:25

Reflecting co-ordinates

RM 62, 1cm squared grid (RM A), glue

The triangle on this grid has been reflected in a mirror line.

The co-ordinates of both triangles are in the chart.

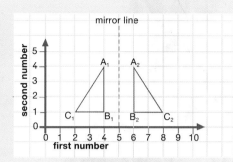

	1st shape		2nd shape	
	point	co-ordinates	point	co-ordinates
	A_1	(4,4)	A_2	(6,4)
	B_1	(4,1)	B_2	(6,1)
	C_1	(2,1)	C_2	(8,1)

1   Carry out the work on RM 62.

2   This grid shows half of a symmetrical shape and mirror line.

- Copy it onto squared paper.
- Mark the reflection of each point and label the reflections A_2, B_2, etc.
- Join the points to complete the shape.
- Cut out the grid and stick it in your book.

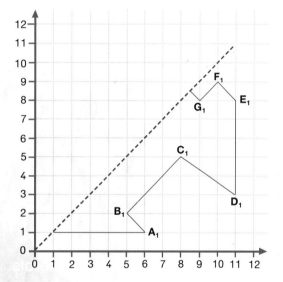

3   Copy and complete this table for your grid.

bottom right		top left	
point	co-ordinates	point	co-ordinates
A_1		A_2	
B_1		B_2	
C_1		C_2	

4   Write about any number patterns you can see in the co-ordinates of the two halves.

5
- Draw another grid like the one for **2** and mark the mirror line.
- Draw a shape in the top left-hand corner, not touching the mirror line.
- Label its points and write its co-ordinates in order.
- Design a table to show what you think the co-ordinates of its reflection will be.
- Then check by drawing the reflection.
- Stick the completed grid in your book.

Transferring shapes

1 Look carefully to see how the shape on the first grid is transferred to the second grid.

2 Use RM 63 to make and transfer your own shape.

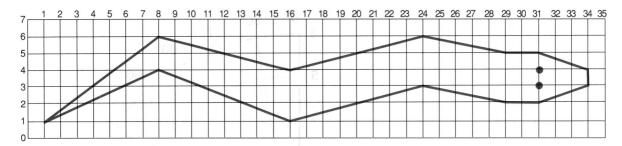

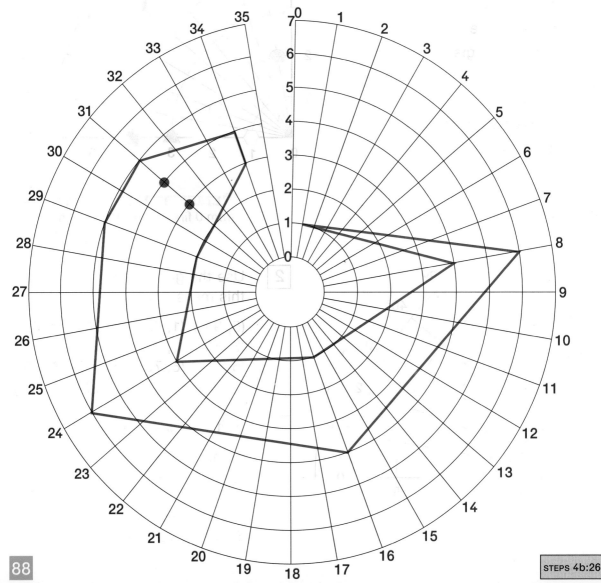

Positions of shapes

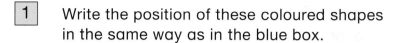

1 Write the position of these coloured shapes in the same way as in the blue box.

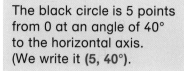

The black circle is 5 points from 0 at an angle of 40° to the horizontal axis. (We write it **(5, 40°)**).

a yellow trapezium
b green square
c blue circle
d black hexagon
e red parallelogram
f yellow circle
g black triangle
h green oblong
i red circle
j red triangle
k yellow parallelogram
l green circle
m blue triangle
n green hexagon

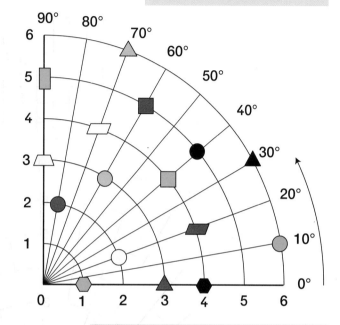

REMEMBER: Write the distance from 0 first, then write the angle.

2 Use the grid to work out this message.

(5, 90°) (1, 90°) (3, 80°) (2, 60°)
(3, 80°) (2, 60°)
(6, 0°) (6, 70°) (5, 60°) (4, 30°)
(6, 70°) (5, 20°) (2, 60°) (4, 30°)

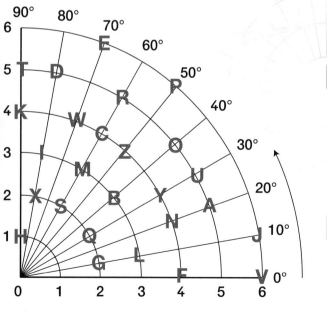

3 Write the codes for:

a the name of your town
b the name of your favourite TV star
c a friend's name
d your favourite food.

Grouping scores

Alison and Shakira ran this darts game at the school fair.

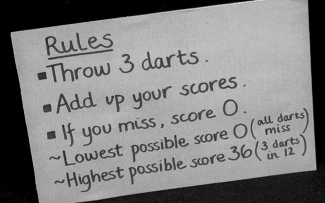

Rules
- Throw 3 darts.
- Add up your scores.
- If you miss, score 0.
~ Lowest possible score 0 (all darts miss)
~ Highest possible score 36 (3 darts in 12)

They wrote down the scores of all the players.

2	31	7	4	5	20	24	16	23	29	15	25
6	24	17	6	12	24	16	10	17	29	15	17
19	36	14	26	21	13	13	13	23	34	15	20
23	21	33	10	22	15	23	20	21	28	21	11

After the fair they organised the scores in a frequency table like this.

This means the five scores of 0, 1, 2, 3 and 4.

Groups of equal numbers of scores like this are called equal class intervals.

frequency table of darts scores

scores	tally	frequency
0 - 4	II	2
5 - 9		
10 - 14		
15 - 19		
20 - 24		
25 - 29		
30 - 34		
35 - 39		

Frequency means the total number of times the scores come up.

1   Copy and complete the frequency table.

2   **a** How many people played the game?
    b Which equal class interval had most scores in it?
    c Which had fewest scores?

Alison and Shakira drew a
frequency diagram of their data.

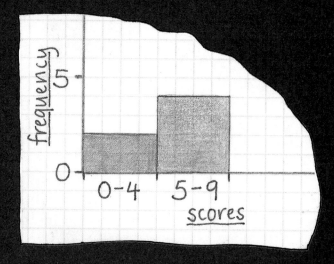

3 Copy and complete their frequency diagram using RM C.

4 Work with four dice and a friend.

■ Roll all four dice 50 times and record the total of your scores each time.
■ Choose equal class intervals and make a frequency table.
■ Draw a frequency diagram of your data.

5 a Which of your class intervals has most scores in it?
   b Which has fewest scores in it?

CHALLENGE

Work with a friend if you can.

■ Decide on a game or topic to explore, and collect data about it.
■ Choose equal class intervals and make a frequency table.
■ Then draw a frequency diagram of the results.

Multiple problems

1 Think of a number to fit each of these.

> The first four multiples of 3 are 3, 6, 9, 12.

   a The smallest multiple of 6 and 8.
   b A multiple of 3 and 4 greater than 20.
   c 10 times a multiple of 5 and 6.

2 ■ Write 10 numbers which are 4 fewer than a multiple of 5.
    ■ Write what is the same about all these numbers.

3 Choose one number from this set: {12, 18, 25, 27, 36, 48, 56, 69, 81, 84} for each lily pad. Make sure it fits all the clues.

a
■ a multiple of 3 and 4
■ a square number
■ 4 less than a multiple of 10

c
■ a multiple of 3
■ 1 less than a multiple of 7
■ greater than 50
■ 5 more than a square number

b
■ a multiple of 2, 3, 4 and 6
■ 3 greater than a multiple of 5
■ 1 less than a square number

4 Copy this diagram and put 5 more numbers in each region.

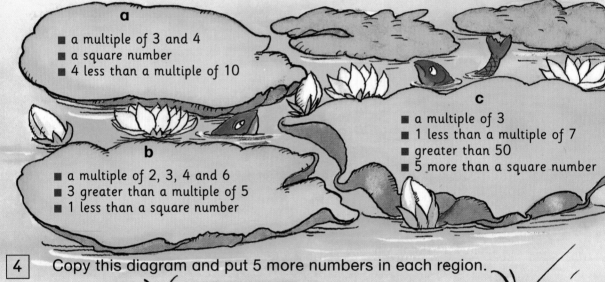

counting numbers

24

3

8

multiples of 6

multiples of 2

50 49 48 47 46 45 44 43 42 41

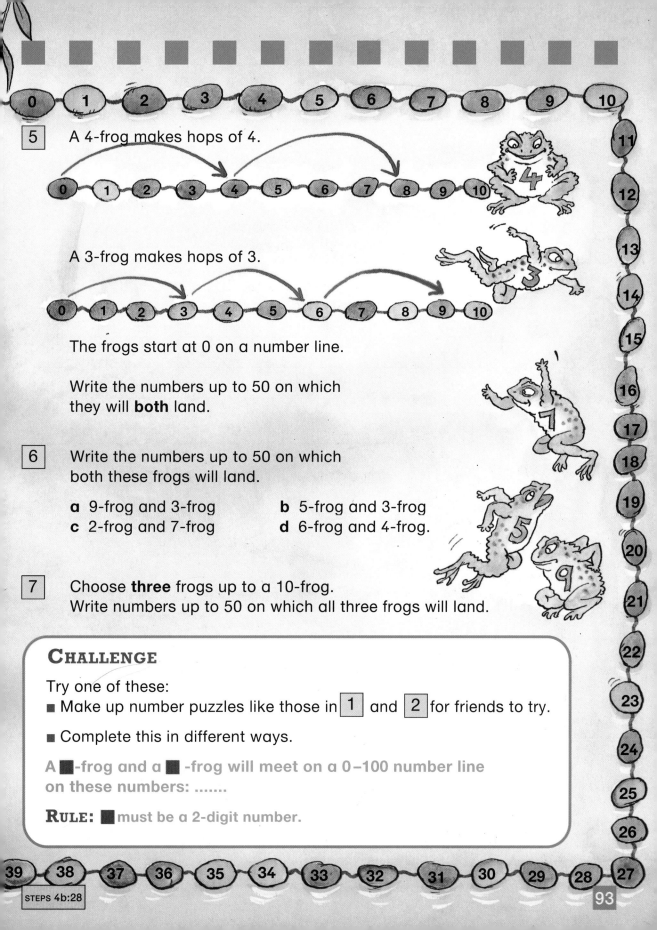

5 A 4-frog makes hops of 4.

A 3-frog makes hops of 3.

The frogs start at 0 on a number line.

Write the numbers up to 50 on which they will **both** land.

6 Write the numbers up to 50 on which both these frogs will land.

a 9-frog and 3-frog   **b** 5-frog and 3-frog
c 2-frog and 7-frog   **d** 6-frog and 4-frog.

7 Choose **three** frogs up to a 10-frog.
Write numbers up to 50 on which all three frogs will land.

CHALLENGE

Try one of these:

■ Make up number puzzles like those in 1 and 2 for friends to try.

■ Complete this in different ways.

A ■-frog and a ■-frog will meet on a 0–100 number line on these numbers: ....

RULE: ■ must be a 2-digit number.

Multiplication grids

■ ■ ■

> I know an easy way of working out 40 x 16 because ...

> ... I know 16 = 10 + 6,
> 40 x 10 = 400
> and 40 x 6 = 240.

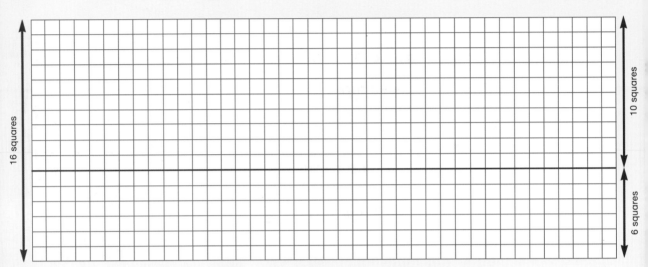

16 squares

10 squares

6 squares

40 × 16 = (40 × 10) + (40 × 6) = 400 + 240 = 640

1 On RM C, draw grids like the one above to work out:

a 30 × 13   **b** 50 × 17   **c** 40 × 32
d 20 × 26   **e** 30 × 34   **f** 50 × 24.

2 Copy and complete.

a 70 × 25 = (70 × 20) + (70 × 5) = 1400 + _____ = _____
b 60 × 42 = (60 × 40) + (60 × 2) = _____ + 120   = _____
c 50 × 53 = (50 × 50) + (50 × 3) = _____ + _____ = _____
d 40 × 71 = (40 × 70) + (40 × 1) = _____ + _____ = _____
e 30 × 42 = (×   ) + (×   ) = _____ + _____ = _____
f 90 × 37 = (×   ) + (×   ) = _____ + _____ = _____

3 Make up more examples like this.

16 x 30 = (10 x 30) + (6 x 30) = 300 + 180 = 480

RULE: ■ must be a 2-digit number. ■ must be a 2-digit multiple of 10.

94

Rows and columns

1 If you buy 2 rows of these stamps, they will cost you
19p x 10 = 190p = £1·90.

Work out the value of the 19p stamps left over.
Give your answer in pounds and pence.

2 Work out the cost of the stamps if you buy:

a 4 rows **b** 10 rows **c** 14 rows **d** 8 rows.

3 Work out the value of the stamps
left after each purchase in 2 .

4 Complete this sentence.
**1 column of stamps costs the same
as .... rows.**

5 Complete this sentence in 4 different ways.
**....... columns of stamps cost the same
as .... rows.**

6 Work out the cost of each set of stamps
if you buy the numbers shown.

a 30    **b** 90

c 60   **d** 50

CHALLENGE

■ Work out different costs if you buy **odd** numbers of rows
from the block of 19p stamps.

■ There are 10 possible answers. Try to find them all.

As the crow flies

On the map, you can measure the distance as the crow flies, between some places in Britain.

'As the crow flies' means 'in a straight line'.

scale

1 cm represents 10 km

STEPS 4b:29

1 Copy and complete this table.

	scaled distance	actual distance
Birmingham to Liverpool	12·3 cm	123 km
Birmingham to Chester		
Birmingham to Sheffield		
Birmingham to Worcester		
Birmingham to Builth Wells		

2 Write the scaled and actual distance between Birmingham and these places.

   a Bradford   **b** Wolverhampton   **c** Colwyn Bay
   d Blackpool   **e** Stoke-on-Trent   **f** Shrewsbury

3 Choose 6 pairs of places which are more than 50 km apart.
(Do not include Birmingham.)
Write the distance in kilometres between each pair.

4 This chart is to show the distance in
kilometres (as the crow flies) between some
places on the map.

It shows that Birmingham and Blackpool
are 162 kilometres apart.

Find the missing distances **a** to **i**.

	Birmingham	Blackpool	Bradford	Builth Wells	Chester
Birmingham					
Blackpool	162				
Bradford	**a**	**b**			
Builth Wells	**c**	**d**	**e**		
Chester	**f**	**g**	**h**	**i**	

CHALLENGE

- Design a distance chart like this
  for five more places from the
  map on page 96.
- Start with Liverpool and continue
  alphabetically.

Driving around

This chart shows the distances, in kilometres, between the same places as on the previous page, **if you drive on the shortest route**.

	Birmingham	Blackpool	Bradford	Builth Wells	Chester	Colwyn Bay
Birmingham						
Blackpool	201					
Bradford	206	132				
Builth Wells	132	253	278			
Chester	125	108	130	148		
Colwyn Bay	193	161	192	193	68	

1 If you were driving, write how many kilometres you would drive from:

  a Builth Wells to Blackpool
  b Colwyn Bay to Bradford
  c Chester to Birmingham
  d Blackpool to Birmingham.

2 Explain why the distances in this chart are longer than those on the chart on page 97.

3 Work out how many kilometres you would drive on these journeys.

  a Birmingham to Colwyn Bay to Bradford
  b Builth Wells to Chester to Blackpool
  c Bradford to Builth Wells to Colwyn Bay
  d Blackpool to Colwyn Bay to Builth Wells to Birmingham

4 Use the chart to help you fill the blanks in this sentence in five different ways. Start at Birmingham.

  If I drive to .... and back, the distance will be ..... km.

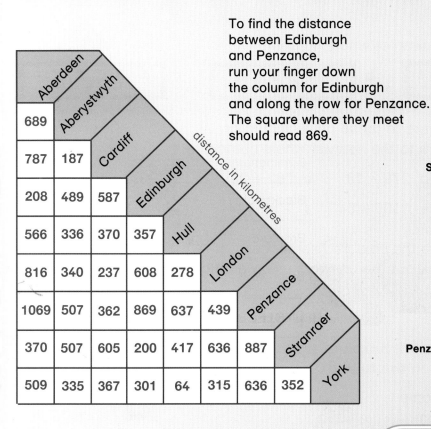

To find the distance between Edinburgh and Penzance, run your finger down the column for Edinburgh and along the row for Penzance. The square where they meet should read 869.

distance in kilometres

Aberdeen	Aberystwyth	Cardiff	Edinburgh	Hull	London	Penzance	Stranraer	York
689								
787	187							
208	489	587						
566	336	370	357					
816	340	237	608	278				
1069	507	362	869	637	439			
370	507	605	200	417	636	887		
509	335	367	301	64	315	636	352	

5 Copy and complete this signpost that might be put up in Hull.

6 Design a signpost like this for 2 other places on the chart.

7 Work out the distance travelled if you make a **return** journey between:

a Penzance and London
b Edinburgh and Cardiff
c Aberdeen and Stranraer
d Hull and Aberystwyth.

Distances	from Hull
Aberdeen	566 km
Aberystwyth	336 km
Cardiff	370 km
Edinburgh	
London	
Penzance	
Stranraer	
York	

CHALLENGE

Complete more sentences like this. **Edinburgh** is **286 km** further from Cardiff than from **York**.

Calculator division

1 Write these to the nearest whole number.

a 516.71 b 82.119 c 7.52164

2 Work out the answers to these on a calculator.
Record the answers to the nearest whole number.

a $146 \div 8$ b $279 \div 18$ c $762 \div 24$

d $450 \div 16$ e $1000 \div 64$ f $214 \div 14$

3 Copy and complete the coloured sentences.
Decide how to work out the answers using a calculator.

a 221 eggs are packed
in boxes of six.
There will be .... full boxes of eggs.
.... eggs will go in the full boxes.

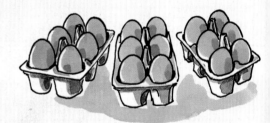

b You have £7 and buy as many
19p stamps as you can.
I can buy .... stamps.
The stamps will cost £ ... · ...
The change will be .... p.

c 327 children and teachers
go on a coach trip. Each coach
takes 45 passengers.
.... coaches will be needed.
There will be .... empty passenger seats.

CHALLENGE

- Using written methods, show that your answers
  to the problems in 3 are correct.
- Show your workings-out.

Decision tree

1 cm squared paper (RM A), scissors

1   Make cards for all numbers 1 to 30 on centimetre squared paper.

2   Find out in which region, A, B, C or D, each card belongs by sliding it along the decision tree from **START** .

3   Record your results for region A like this.
Set of numbers for region A = {10, ___, ___}

4   Do the same for regions B, C and D.

5   Explain how the numbers in each region are the same.

6   Write other numbers you could put in each region.

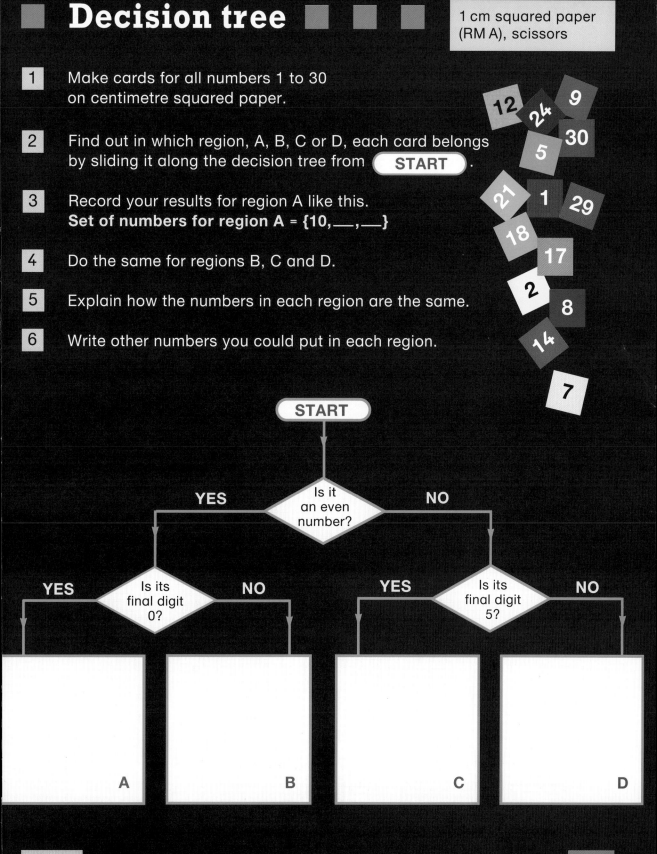

START

Is it an even number?

YES   NO

Is its final digit 0?

YES   NO

Is its final digit 5?

YES   NO

A   B   C   D

Multiples of 9 and 3

1 Write 6 numbers less than 100 which are exactly divisible by 9.

> Numbers such as 5, 20 and 75 are exactly divisible by 5.
> They are **multiples** of 5.

2 Use your calculator to find 6 numbers exactly divisible by 9 in this set.
Write them down.

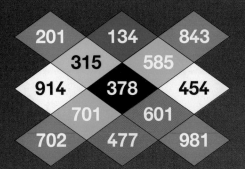

3 ▪ Draw a table like this.
▪ List your multiples of 9 from **1** and **2** on it in ascending order.
▪ Complete it.

> To find the **digital sum** of a number, add its digits.
> $312 \longrightarrow 3 + 1 + 2 = \mathbf{6}$
> $68 \longrightarrow 6 + 8 = 14 \longrightarrow 1 + 4 = \mathbf{5}$

multiple of 9	digital sum

4 Without working out the answers, write which of these you think are multiples of 9.

936   **144**   **675**

702   **571**

443

5 Without working out the answers, write:

a 6 numbers greater than 1000 divisible by 9
b 6 numbers greater than 1000 **not** divisible by 9.

Check your answers with a calculator.

6 Explain how you recognise a multiple of 9.

7 Write 6 numbers less than 100, exactly divisible by 3.

8 Use your calculator to find 9 numbers exactly divisible by 3 in this star.

Write them down.

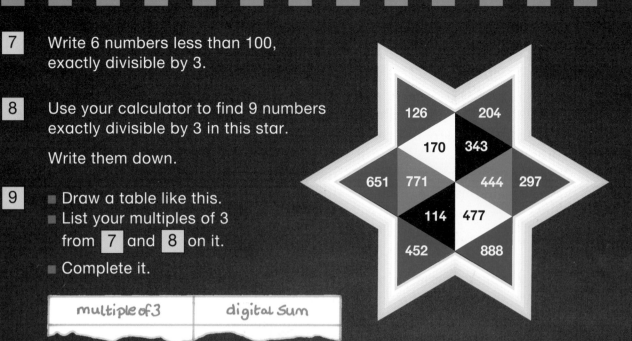

126   204
170   343
651   771   444   297
114   477
452   888

9 ■ Draw a table like this.
  ■ List your multiples of 3 from 7 and 8 on it.
  ■ Complete it.

multiple of 3	digital sum

10 Without working out the answers, write which of these you think are multiples of 3.

351   132   117   913   404   831

11 Without working out the answers, write:

  a 6 numbers greater than 1000 divisible by 3
  b 6 numbers greater than 1000 **not** divisible by 3.

12 Explain how you can recognise a multiple of 3.

CHALLENGE

■ Put numbers in each of these regions.
■ Explain how you can recognise if a number is divisible by 6 without working out the answer.

multiple of 6	not a multiple of 6

Symmetry patterns

1cm squared paper
(RM A), scissors

1
- Draw these two shapes on squared paper and cut them out.
- Arrange them so that they touch to make shapes that have a **line of symmetry**.
- Make as many **different** arrangements as you can.
- Record your patterns on squared paper, marking the lines of symmetry.

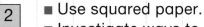

2
- Use squared paper.
- Investigate ways to arrange 6 linked squares to make a symmetrical pattern.
- Mark the lines of symmetry. Here are some.

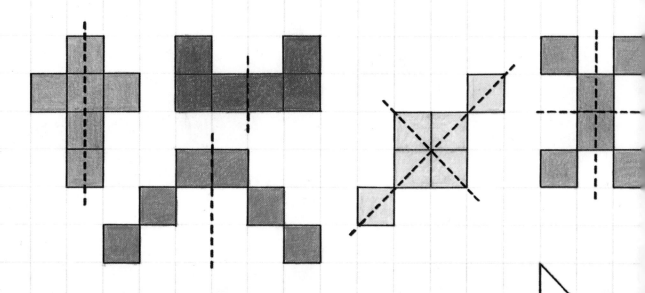

3
- Draw this shape in the middle of a piece of squared paper.
- Add squares and half squares so that it has **reflective symmetry** and an area of 8 square centimetres.
- Colour the shape.
- Repeat this five more times. Make sure that all 6 shapes have reflective symmetry.

Symmetry puzzle

mirror

1 Use a mirror on this shape to make shapes **a** to **j**.

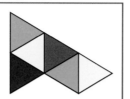

a

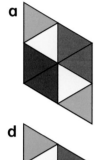

b

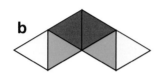

c

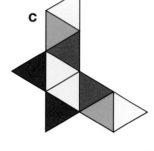

d

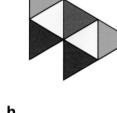

e **f** **g**

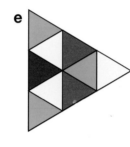

h

i

j

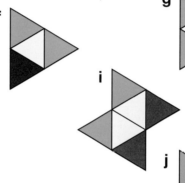

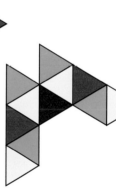

CHALLENGE

Find these shapes
using the mirror
and the shape
at the top of the page.

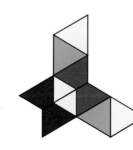

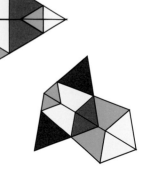

interlocking cubes

A **plane** is a flat surface, like a wall or a mirror.
A plane that splits a 3-D shape into
two exactly matching halves
is called a **plane of symmetry**.

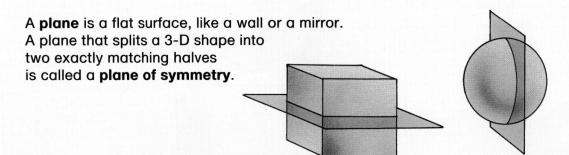

1 Do these show planes of symmetry? Write Yes or No.

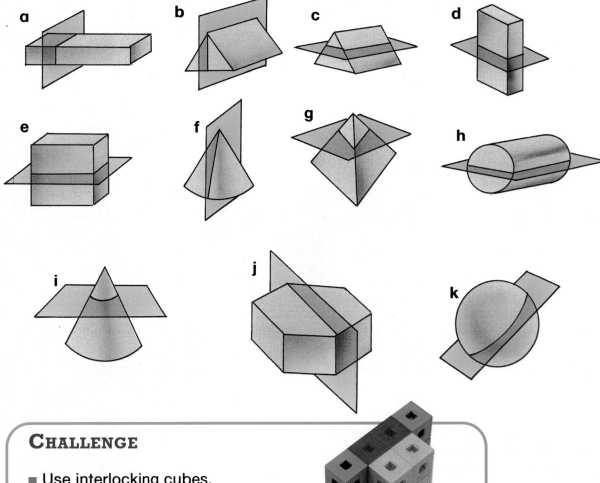

a

b

c

d

e

f

g

h

i

j

k

CHALLENGE

■ Use interlocking cubes.
■ Make different shapes
that show two **planes of symmetry**.

STEPS 4b:31

Millilitres and cm³

250 ml measuring cylinder, Plasticine

Work with a friend if you can.

1
- Pour water into the measuring cylinder up to the 100 ml mark.
- Make a shape using 20 Centicubes.
- Put the shape in the water and record the new water level.

2 Repeat **1** using shapes of the volume shown in this chart.
Copy and complete the chart to show your results.

Volume of shape	Starting water level	New water level	Amount of rise of water level
20 cu cm	100 ml	ml	ml
30 cu cm	100 ml	ml	ml
40 cu cm	100 ml	ml	ml
50 cu cm	100 ml	ml	ml
60 cu cm	100 ml	ml	ml

3 Write what you notice about the numbers in the first and last columns.

4 Copy and complete these sentences:

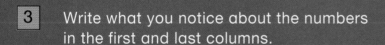
- I predict that a 100 cu cm shape will make the water rise by _____ ml.
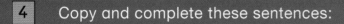
- I predict that a 1 cu cm shape will make the water level rise by _____ ml.

CHALLENGE

- Use small objects, like pebbles or lumps of Plasticine, water and a measuring cylinder.
- Decide the best way to find the volume of each object.

What's the capacity?

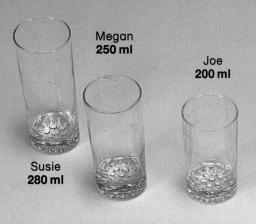

Megan
250 ml

Joe
200 ml

Susie
280 ml

Lucy
180 ml

1 litre

Tariq
320 ml

1 What is the total quantity of juice needed to fill Tariq's and Megan's glasses?

2 Whose glass holds:

a most   **b** least   **c** the median amount? (See page 68 for 'median'.)

3 How much more does Tariq's glass hold than Lucy's?

4 Which four glasses would you have to fill to leave 50 ml in the bottle?

5 How many full glasses could you pour from the bottle using:

a Joe's glass   **b** Tariq's glass   **c** Megan's glass
d Susie's glass   **e** Lucy's glass?

6 Find out how much juice would be left in the bottle after each pouring in **5**. Like this for Joe's glass:

a 1000 ml ⟶ 800 ml ⟶ 600 ml ⟶ 400 ml ⟶ 200 ml ⟶ 0 ml left.

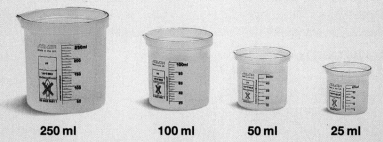

250 ml   100 ml   50 ml   25 ml

7 **a** If you poured **one or more** of these measured amounts of water into an empty litre container, show that you could make 10 different amounts.
b How much space would be left in the litre container each time?

Use a jug, a cup and a glass.

8 Fill the jug to the top calibration.

   a Estimate how many times the jug could fill the cup.
   b Check your estimate.

9 **a** Estimate how many times the jug
      could fill the glass.
   b Check your estimate.

10 **a** Could you fill more cups or more glasses?
   b Which holds more, the cup or the glass?
   c Write about how you chose your answers.

11 ■ Choose 5 friends and estimate
      the capacity of each person's left hand.
   ■ Use loose Centicubes
      to compare the capacities.

CHALLENGE

Work with a friend if you can.
■ Use uncalibrated containers
  of different sizes and
  a measuring jug.
■ Estimate, then find the capacity
  of each container if you fill it
  with water to a level 1 cm below
  its brim.

RULES
■ Do your measuring by pouring water **from** the jug
  to the container.
■ Afterwards, check your measurements
  by pouring the water back into the measuring jug.

Pyramids

templates of squares and regular pentagons, card, compasses, glue, scissors, RM H

The Great Pyramid contains
2 300 000 blocks of stone.
Each block weighs 2 500 kilograms.
It was originally 146·6 metres high.

The pyramids of Giza in Egypt were built over 3 000 years ago. What kind of pyramids are they?

1. Make this net for a **square-based** pyramid.

   ■ Draw the outline of a square on card.
     (5 cm sides is a good size.)
   ■ Construct an equilateral triangle
     on each side.

   Look at page 19 if you can't
   remember what to do.

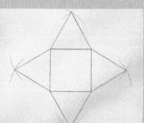

2. Add a tab (1 cm wide) to each triangle
   and cut out the net.

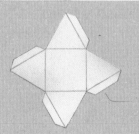

3. Score along the fold lines, and
   fold the net up to make sure it fits together.
   Then glue each tab in turn.

STEPS 4b:33

4 Use a stencil of a regular pentagon (with sides of 5 cm or more) to help you complete a net like this for a **pentagonal** pyramid. Repeat [2] and [3] to complete it.

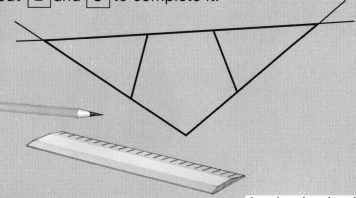

5 Copy this net of a **hexagonal** pyramid onto a card copy of RM H. Complete it in the same way as the others.

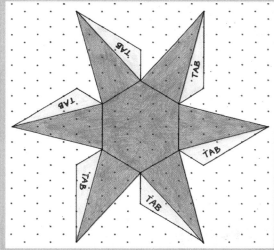

6 Copy and complete this table.

7 Write how many faces, edges and vertices pyramids with these bases will have.

base of pyramid	faces	edges	vertices
triangle			
square			
pentagon			
hexagon			

a octagon   **b** decagon

8 Describe how all the pyramids you have made are the same.

3-D sorts

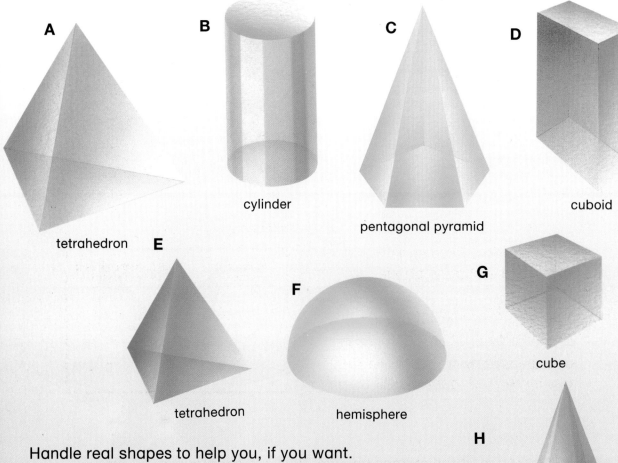

A tetrahedron

B cylinder

C pentagonal pyramid

D cuboid

E tetrahedron

F hemisphere

G cube

H cone

Handle real shapes to help you, if you want.

1   Write the letter of the shape being described.
     Choose from those shown on both pages.

   a It's the only shape with no flat surfaces.
   b It won't roll in a straight line.
   c It has 5 faces, but none of them is oblong.
   d It has 6 vertices but isn't a prism.
   e It has 8 edges. Four of its faces are congruent to each other.
   f It has the same number of right-angled corners as a cuboid.
     All its faces are congruent to each other. It is the smaller
     of two on display.
   g It has 6 fewer edges than a cube. It has 12 acute angles. It isn't blue.

2   Write clues for these shapes.

   a blue cuboid   **b** hemisphere   **c** cylinder   **d** larger cube

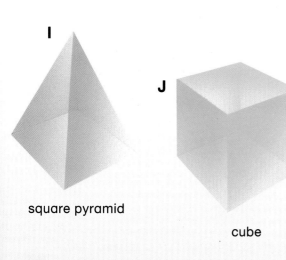

I

J

square pyramid

cube

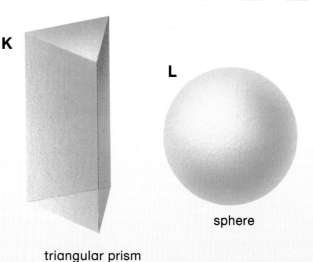

K

L

sphere

triangular prism

3 Complete RM 77 to sort some of the shapes above.

4 Write in which region, 1 to 8, you would put these shapes.

a triangular prism   **b** cylinder
c sphere   **d** pentagonal pyramid

| at least five faces | all faces congruent to each other |

1   2   3
4   5   6
7
blue   8

CHALLENGE

Write the letters of the shapes you would put in each region coloured **red**.

a
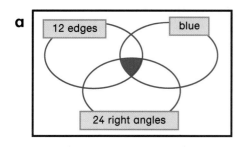
12 edges · blue · 24 right angles

b
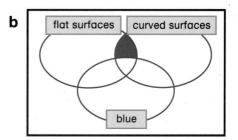
flat surfaces · curved surfaces · blue

c
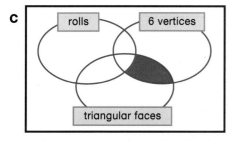
rolls · 6 vertices · triangular faces

d
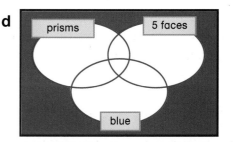
prisms · 5 faces · blue

Lorry journeys ■ ■ ■ ■ ■

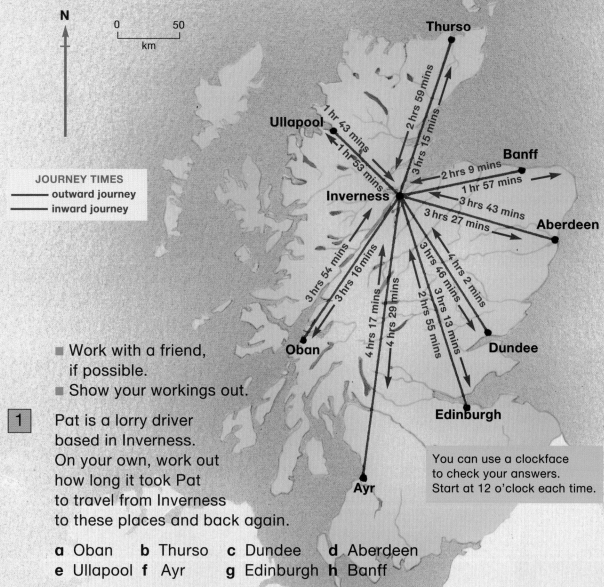

N

JOURNEY TIMES
— outward journey
— inward journey

Thurso

Ullapool
1 hr 43 mins
1 hr 53 mins
2 hrs 59 mins
3 hrs 15 mins

Banff
2 hrs 9 mins
1 hr 57 mins
3 hrs 43 mins
3 hrs 27 mins

Inverness

Aberdeen

3 hrs 54 mins
3 hrs 16 mins
4 hrs 17 mins
4 hrs 29 mins
2 hrs 55 mins
3 hrs 46 mins
3 hrs 13 mins
4 hrs 2 mins

Oban

Dundee

Edinburgh

Ayr

0 50
km

- Work with a friend, if possible.
- Show your workings out.

1 Pat is a lorry driver based in Inverness. On your own, work out how long it took Pat to travel from Inverness to these places and back again.

You can use a clockface to check your answers. Start at 12 o'clock each time.

a Oban **b** Thurso **c** Dundee **d** Aberdeen
e Ullapool **f** Ayr **g** Edinburgh **h** Banff

When each of you has an answer, compare them. If you get different answers, try to find out why.

2 Complete this sentence in at least 8 different ways.
... hours ... minutes and ... hours ... minutes make 5 hours.

CHALLENGE

Together, work out the mean (average) of the outward and inward times for each journey in **1**. (Page 70 will remind you about the mean.)

Trip plan ■ ■ ■ ■ ■ ■

A Day Trip to FUTURE WORLD Theme Park

Bus

To FUTURE WORLD

depart	arrive
09:04	09:44
09:22	10:03
09:52	10:32

From FUTURE WORLD

depart	arrive
14:40	15:20
14:58	15:42
15:14	15:56

5 minutes walk
to the Theme Park.

Train

To FUTURE WORLD

depart	arrive
09:17	09:47
09:55	10:25
10:42	11:09

From FUTURE WORLD

depart	arrive
14:59	15:31
15:09	15:39
15:17	15:47

OPEN
Weekdays
10:30~18:30
Weekends
8:30~21:00

10 minutes walk
to the Theme Park.

Work with a partner, if you can.

1 Plan a day out for your class at the Future World Theme Park.
  ■ You cannot leave school before 9.15 am
    and you must be back by 4.00 pm.

  ■ You can either travel by train or by bus. The bus stop is 10 minutes
    walk from school or you could walk to the train station in $\frac{1}{4}$ hour.

  ■ Work out the different possible travel arrangements.

  ■ Show your preferred time-table for the day.
    Write about the reasons for your choices.
    Say how long you will be able to spend at the park.

■ TV times ■ ■ ■ ■ ■ ■ ■

Work with a partner if you can.

1
- ■ You want to record these television programmes to watch later.
- ■ You have two empty video tapes, one of 180 minutes and one of 240 minutes.
- ■ Investigate the best way to fit the programmes on the tapes.

CARTOON MAGIC
Thursday 7th
From **09:05** to **09:20**

SPARKS
Friday 8th
From **18:10** to **19:15**

TIGER'S EYE
Tuesday 5th
From **15:05** to **16:30**

STARBURST
Monday 4th
From **14:10** to **15:10**

THE DARK SECRET
Sunday 10th
From **12:05** to **13:25**

DRAGON RACE
Saturday 9th
From **18:20** to **20:05**

1
Record your choices on two tables like these.

180-minute video				
Programme	Date	Start time	Finish time	Duration
				Total duration:

240-minute video				
Programme	Date	Start time	Finish time	Duration
				Total duration:

Function machines

1 Copy these function machine tables and fill in the outputs.
Try to work them out in your head.

a

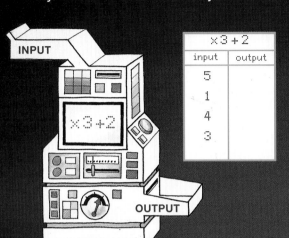

INPUT

OUTPUT

×3 + 2	
input	output
5	
1	
4	
3	

×9 − 3	
input	output
8	
9	
7	
5	

b

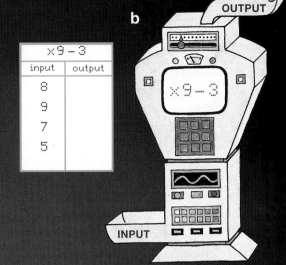

OUTPUT

INPUT

c

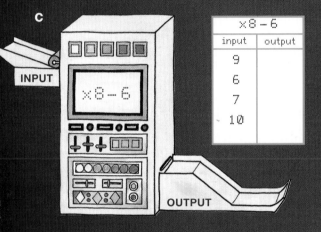

INPUT

OUTPUT

×8 − 6	
input	output
9	
6	
7	
10	

− 6 ×8	
input	output
9	
6	
7	
10	

d

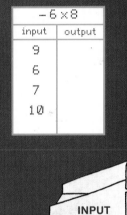

OUTPUT

INPUT

2 Make up your own 2-operation machines
like these. Try changing the order of operations.
Does the order of the operations matter?

CHALLENGE

- Choose a number.
- If it is odd, add 1.
- If it is even, divide by 2.
- Keep doing this. **What happens**?
- Try it with other numbers.

If you chose 67, you would start like this:
67 → 68 → 34 → 17 → 18 ...

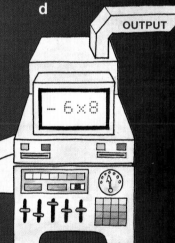

Put odd numbers through me.

Put even numbers through me.

IN OUT
+1

IN OUT
÷2

What is the number?

■ ■ ■ ■

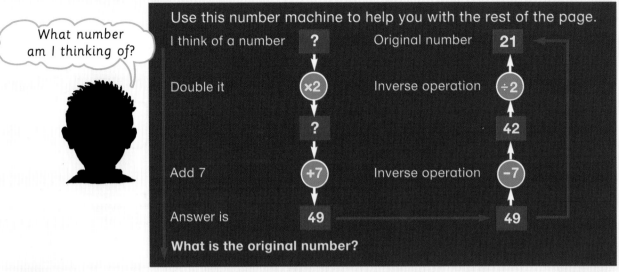

What number am I thinking of?

Use this number machine to help you with the rest of the page.

I think of a number	?	Original number	21
Double it	×2	Inverse operation	÷2
	?		42
Add 7	+7	Inverse operation	−7
Answer is	49		49

What is the original number?

1 Check that 21 is correct by putting it through the left side of the machine.

2 Find the answers to these using the number machine method.

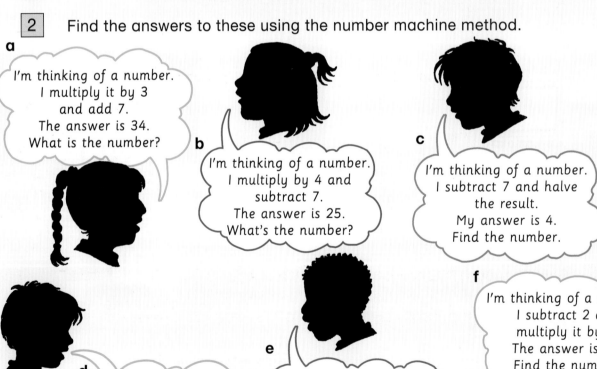

a

I'm thinking of a number.
I multiply it by 3
and add 7.
The answer is 34.
What is the number?

b

I'm thinking of a number.
I multiply by 4 and
subtract 7.
The answer is 25.
What's the number?

c

I'm thinking of a number.
I subtract 7 and halve
the result.
My answer is 4.
Find the number.

d

I'm thinking of a number.
I halve it and add 9.
The answer is 34.
What's the number?

e

I'm thinking of a number.
I subtract 5.
I divide by 5.
My answer is 5.
What's the number?

f

I'm thinking of a numb[er]
I subtract 2 and
multiply it by 3.
The answer is 30.
Find the number.

3 Show how you can check that each answer in **2** is correct.

Garden patterns

Investigate mathematics in the garden.

1 post   0 panels

2 posts   1 panel

3 posts   2 panels

1   Draw simple diagrams to represent this fence. Draw the next 3 diagrams.

2   **a** Copy and complete this table for the diagrams you have drawn.

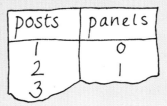

posts	panels
1	0
2	1
3	

b Choose an operation box for your table from the ones at the bottom of the page.

input posts output panels

3   Repeat steps **1** and **2** for this fence:

1 post   0 bars

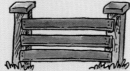

2 posts   3 bars

3 posts   6 bars

4   Repeat steps **1** and **2** for these flower beds:

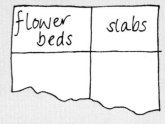

flower beds	slabs

> **Remember:** The operation must link every input to its output number.

×2+3   ×2+6   ×3−3   +3×3   −1   +3×2

Tessellation and angles

Here are 3 congruent isoceles triangles.

The triangles tessellate like this:

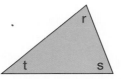 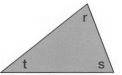 

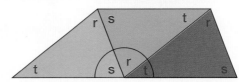

1 Copy and complete
The 3 angles of an .... triangle together make .... degrees.

2 ■ Use 3 congruent triangles from each of these families:
   a scalene   **b** right-angled   **c** equilateral.
■ Show that you can arrange them in the same way.
■ Write a sentence like the **blue** one about each kind of triangle.

4 kites congruent to this one ...   ... can tessellate like this.

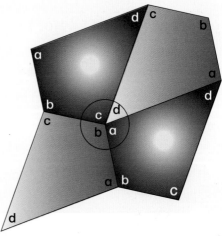

3 Copy and complete
The 4 angles of a .... together make .... degrees.

4 ■ Use 4 congruent shapes from each of these families:
   a parallelograms   **b** trapezia   **c** quadrilaterals (no equal sides).
■ Show that you can arrange them in the same way.
■ Write a sentence like the **red** one about each kind of quadrilateral.

5 Explain why the angles of squares and oblongs total 360°.

STEPS 4b:36

Tessellating hexagon

hexagon template, card, sticky tape, scissors, large sheets of paper

1. ■ Use the template to cut a regular hexagon out of card Cut from one corner to another like this. →

   ■ Translate the cut-out piece to the opposite side and tape it in place. →

   ■ Cut another piece from one side translate it to the opposite side and tape it in place. →

   ■ Repeat 'cut, translate, tape' on another side. →

2. Draw round your shape and make it tessellate.

3. Decorate your design.

Half-side rotation

pieces of card,
sticky tape, scissors,
large sheets of paper

1 ■ Cut out a quadrilateral and mark
the mid-point of each side.

■ Cut away a piece from half of one side,
rotate it about the mid-point
and fix it to the uncut half.
Show that this new shape will tessellate.

■ Repeat the process from another side.
Be sure to keep the cut-out piece flat
as you rotate it.

Show that this shape will tessellate.

■ If you like, you can repeat the process again
for the other two sides.

2 Draw round your
shape and make
it tessellate.

3 Decorate your design.